WOMAN'S DAY
SERVING FOOD WITH STYLE

WOMAN'S
SERVING

DAY
FOOD WITH STYLE

by Carole Collier

DOUBLEDAY & COMPANY, INC.
GARDEN CITY, NEW YORK

*For my Dad,
Alexander E. Mielnikowski*

Library of Congress Cataloging in Publication Data

Collier, Carole.
  Woman's day serving food with style.

  Includes index.
  1. Food presentation.   2. Entertaining.
3. Cookery.   I. Woman's day.   II. Title.
TX652.C713   1982   642
ISBN 0-385-18517-0   AACR2
Library of Congress Catalog Card Number 81–43116

Copyright © 1981, 1982 by CBS Consumer Publishing,
A Division of CBS Inc.
All rights reserved
Printed in the United States of America

Design by Jeanette Portelli

Contents

Foreword   The Importance of Food Presentation   ix

Food for Thought   xiii

1. The Strategies of Food Presentation   1

Attitude   1
Helping Hands   1
The Pleasurable and Memorable Sense of Smell   2
Taste   3
Texture   3
Color   5
The Cook's Color Chart   8
Lighting   12

2. Kitchen Equipment   15

Gadgets and Tools   16

APPLE CORER • APPLE AND PEAR DIVIDER • ASPIC, GARNISHING, AND TRUFFLE CUTTERS • BIRD'S-NEST MAKER • BOUQUET GARNI BAGS • BUTTER CURLERS • BUTTER PADDLES • CHERRY AND OLIVE PITTER • CITRUS SCORER AND STRIPPER • CITRUS SHELLER • CITRUS ZESTER • EGG RINGS • EGG SLICER • EGG WEDGER • GRATERS • GRINDERS AND MILLS • HONEY DIPPER • ICE CREAM SCOOPS • LEMON WEDGE BAGS • MEAT FRILLS • MELON-BALL CUTTERS • MUSHROOM BRUSH • MUSHROOM FLUTER • PASTRY BAGS • PASTRY WHEEL •

PIE BIRD • PIE SPATULA • PIE WEIGHTS • PINEAPPLE CUTTER • RADISH ROSETTE PRESS • RADISH SPIRAL CUTTER • ROLLING MINCER • SHRIMP CLEANERS • STRAWBERRY HULLER • TOMATO CUTTER • VEGETABLE PEELERS • WONDERBALL • ZUCCHINI CORER.

Culinary Molds 48

STORE-BOUGHT • INDIVIDUAL • BABA OR TIMBALE • BRIOCHE • EGG EN GELÉE RAMEKINS • ICE SCULPTURE • SAVARIN OR RING-SHAPED • BUTTER • CROQUE MONSIEUR TOASTING IRON • GELATIN OR ICE CREAM • PÂTÉ.

Knives 59

PARING • CHEF'S • SLICING OR CARVING • SERRATED • BONING • FLUTED • GRAPEFRUIT • ZIGZAG OR V-KNIFE.

3. Setting Pretty 64

Table Napery 65

Plate Service 73

Flatware 75

Centerpiece Ideas 76

Multifunctional Tableware 79

BASKETS • BOTTLES • BOWLS • CAKE PLATE • CARAFES • CHAFING DISH • COFFEE AND TEA ACCOUTERMENTS • COLANDER • COOKIE JAR • CUTTING BOARD • EGG CUPS • STUFFED-EGG PLATE • GLASSES • ICE BUCKET OR WINE COOLER • PITCHERS • PLATTERS • PUNCH BOWL SET • SCALLOP SHELLS • SUGAR BOWL AND CREAMER • TUREEN.

4. Foods, Plain and Fancy 92

Bread 93

Butter or Margarine 93

HERB • SAVORY • VEGETABLE • BREAKFAST OR DESSERT • CANAPÉ • SNACK • RED WINE • FLOWER BUTTERS.

Cakes 95

Casseroles 97

Chocolate   97
   CHOCOLATE LEAVES   98

Coffee   99
Condiments   100
Fish   100
Frankfurters   101
   SWISS • PIZZA • CHEF'S SALAD • MACARONI AND FRANK SALAD • GLAZED FRANKS • FRENCH • DUTCH • FRANKS ESPAGNOLE • PITA FRANKS • HOG DOG • DIXIE DOG • SOPHISTICATED FRANK • GARDEN DOG • BREAKFAST FRANK • FRANKLY DELIGHTFUL • TEX-MEX DOG.

Fruit Fillips   102
Garnishes   104
   VEGETABLE CUPS • CITRUS WEDGES • PICKLE FANS • RADISH ROSES • CELERY CURLS • CARROT CURLS • FROSTED FRUITS • ONION CHRYSANTHEMUMS • JULIENNE VEGETABLES • VEGETABLE BASKETS • TOMATO ROSES • ORANGE BUTTERFLIES • ORANGE LOOPS • FLOWERS.

Hamburgers   110
   HANDY BURGER • INTERNATIONAL • REUBEN • TACO • CALIFORNIA • HAWAIIAN • SCRAMBLED • BURGER QUEEN • GREEK • CANADIAN • BIG APPLEBURGER • NEW ENGLAND • RUSSIAN • ITALIAN • DELI BURGER • INDIAN • PIZZA • SPINACH • FAVORITE BURGER.

Ice Ideas   111
Meat and Poultry   112
Oils   113
Pastry Dough   114
Pie Crimping   114
Potatoes   116
Rice   117
Salads   118

Salad Toppings 121
    NUTS • SEEDS • BREAKFAST CEREALS • CROUTONS OR TOASTED BREAD CUBES • FRESH HERBS • VEGETABLE TRIMMINGS • SPROUTS • FRESH FRUIT • CANNED FRUIT • DRIED FRUIT • FRESH VEGETABLES • CANNED VEGETABLES • PICKLES AND GARNITURES • MEATS • FISH • EGGS • CHEESE.

Sandwiches 123
    TOASTED CHEESE ROLL-UPS • ROLLED SANDWICHES • WAFFLE • PINWHEEL • CHECKERBOARD FINGER SANDWICHES • CLUB • MINIATURE • OPEN-FACE • TREASURE CHEST OF SANDWICHES • FROSTED SANDWICH CAKE.

Soups 132
Tea 132
Vegetable Fillips 134
Vinegars 137
Miscellaneous Hints 138

5. Eventful Ideas 139

Breakfast 139
Canned Chic 142
Children's Meals 144
Diet Delights 145
Invalid Meals 148
Hot Weather Food 149
Independence Day—Red, White, and Blue Foods 151
Picnics 152
Wine and Cheese Tasting 154
Meals for One 155

Index 157

Foreword
The Importance of Food Presentation

The need for nourishment and the desire for pleasure are primitive sensations that have been coupled together since the civilization of mankind. When we think about eating we think about all the enjoyable sensations that surround food. Aromas, tastes, colors, and textures, as well as ambiance, décor, comfort, and conviviality, all contribute to the enjoyment. When these elements combine harmoniously, dining becomes a fulfilling and total pleasure. It is this experience that makes our food more than just what we eat.

Food is a vehicle of expression. It can reflect our life styles, cultural styles, and traditions, as well as offer a means of showing or withholding love.

Food has the ability to gratify all our senses. When it is pleasing, food nourishes the spirit as well as the body.

Food can satisfy us in innumerable ways when these special attributes are truly understood. The key to achieving multiple benefits from food lies in the thoughtful presentation of each meal, no matter what the time of day. It only takes a little caring and imagination. Try to remember that the presentation of food mirrors the cook's heart and soul, and that the way a meal is set out conveys a first impression that will either dampen or delight the diner's expectations. A conscientious presentation can set a stage by alerting the instincts and whetting the appetite, thus creating a multisensory chain reaction. Yet this is not complicated.

It's true that we are living at an accelerated pace and that most people don't have as much time to devote to food preparation as they might have had in the past. That's why this book has been written. It's not an ordinary cookbook. It's more of an idea book, a handy guide that's been designed for speedy reference to stimulate your mind and spark your imagination. By learning how to present your meals creatively, you will be able to share a rewarding experience with those you love.

Food presentation, after all, is not just simply a matter of decorating platters. Color, texture, and flavor combinations, quantity and arrangement of food, choice of containers, table appointments, and lighting are all part of the ambiance that makes eating a pleasurable experience. When these factors have been carefully considered and when casualness has been combined with elegance, food presentation becomes a visual and sensual art form. This art entails:

• Thought and planning—simple guidelines have been laid out on these pages to aid you in achieving a firm understanding of food presentation and how it may be used to your best advantage.

• Kitchen equipment—gadgets and tools that turn simple foods into special morsels have been itemized for quick and easy reference.

• Eclectic confidence—a separate chapter on tableware and table dressings suggests ways of using your ordinary household items in unexpected, extraordinary ways to surprise and delight your family and guests, and to please yourself.

• Construction of contrasts in colors, shapes, textures, and tastes—a detailed food chapter thoroughly describes unique ways of handling and utilizing many types of food.

• Creative stimulation—ideas have been gathered to lend originality to special-occasion or everyday events.

As with other art forms, the success of food presentation ultimately depends on personal style and imagination. These traits, however, can be sharpened and developed from the foundations we have built into the pages of this book.

✻

The Importance of Food Presentation

There's an old saying, "Food should feed the eyes first." That simple statement, today, has more meaning than ever before. Food trends, styles, and eating habits have changed, for better and worse, to such a degree that our entire meal strategy bears rethinking.

Recent surveys show that togetherness at the family table is on the decline. Many family members are so involved with events outside the home that breakfast, lunch, or dinner is eaten on a catch-as-catch-can basis. By applying a little of the creative knowledge that can be found in the pages of this book, you will be able to make those meals that are shared with your family into special events that will be cherished. Just a few thoughtful touches in the way your food is presented can make a world of difference and turn the occasion into one of joy, warmth, and happiness.

Modern circumstances have also affected the increasing number of one-parent families. With that one parent often out working or perhaps dating, and baby sitters taking over the feeding chores, this reduced family does not have many opportunities to enjoy meals together. Yet an important element for both parent and children in such a situation is a secure feeling of love. Many single parents can turn to shared meals as a way of being together and exchanging the news of the day. A child and a single parent can cook together, create together, and enjoy a closer relationship through food. Preparing a meal and enjoying it with your child provides an opportunity to talk and laugh and remind one another that you are a family.

The same can be said about cooking for two. Two people who create a meal together are involved in a basic human ritual that can reinforce a bond between them. The way the food is prepared and presented is an expression of love and kinship.

The gradually increasing involvement of men in food-related activities is on the upgrade in American families today. Men are involved in the shopping, preparation, and cleaning up, and they are feeling the enjoyment, pride, and accomplishment that come from cooking. They are interested and they care about what is going on in the kitchen. Even when they aren't doing the cooking they are showing a growing appreciation for the role of food in their lives. It's a wonderful opportunity to participate in a family activity, to turn what might have been a daily routine into a creative event, to add those imaginative touches that make food special.

More and more people are eating alone, either because they live alone or because of family schedules. A meal or a snack for one person needn't be a dreary event. With a bit of imagination and flair, it can be a delight to the eye and the taste buds. A brown-bag lunch, a tray for someone ill, a ready-prepared meal to be eaten in your absence, or your own breakfast in bed will be appreciated and enjoyed much more if it is presented in a way that appeals to the artistic nature as well as the appetite. Whether you prepare meals for yourself on a regular basis or only once in a while, there's no reason why you can't make a creative ritual out of arranging the simplest of ingredients. Eating alone becomes a joy when you make an effort to be inventive with food. It doesn't take extra time and there's no mystery to it. All it requires is the basic knowledge this book will give you, plus a new attitude about the presentation of food.

Americans are becoming health conscious—we're jogging or swimming or playing tennis to keep trim, and we're careful of what and how much we eat. The word "diet" weaves its way in and out of our lives, bringing to mind pangs of agony and deprivation. How is it possible to sustain ourselves and at the same time remain on a diet when we're dissatisfied with every mouthful? Create a diversion! A small effort can be made to delight and entice your senses—those of sight, smell, and touch. You can learn to compensate for what is lacking in the taste of ordinary diet foods by skillfully using color and design, aroma and textures in these special meals. Body-beautiful farms, for example, have become very profitable businesses in the United States. One of the main reasons for their success is that the food they provide, however simple or low in calories, is always served with style and flair. There's no doubt that, on any diet (health or reducing), the way the food is presented is the secret to enjoying the meal. With a few tricks tucked under your toque, you just might stay on that diet as long as you'd like to and be happy as well.

※

These are but a few examples of the ways in which our modern age has changed our relationship to food. It's quite obvious that food is not just mere fuel-for-living. It's a way of expressing what we feel and what we are or what we'd like to be. If we learn how to apply it to our advantage, we can use it to enhance our lives and reap many benefits from it.

Most everyone in our society has learned how to cook to some extent. Now it's time to go one step further. Where most cookbooks leave off, this one begins.

The Importance of Food Presentation

A cook with the most limited culinary skills can learn how to present the simplest foods with style and pride. Those who don't have the time to cook lavishly can dress their fare to create an illusion or style, and those who are experienced will find new and rewarding ideas for offering their repertoire. Whatever your cooking acumen, this book is intended to spur your creativity in presenting foods imaginatively and the end result will add interest and excitement to your meals. Some of the suggestions may motivate you to new ideas of your own.

The pages that follow are designed for the busy person, whether they are full-time homemakers or not. Hundreds of variations are presented in concise form so that you will find the book easy to use. We hope you'll enjoy it and that it makes your cooking more delightful and rewarding.

※

Food for Thought

On the following pages you will find hundreds of descriptions of food presentations. You might, for example, read about golden fried chicken served on a turquoise-blue platter garnished with fresh orange blossoms. Each description is written very precisely in order to help you visualize colorful images as you read. Once you are accustomed to thinking about food presentation in terms of specific color combinations, physical shapes, textures, flavors, and aromas, you can allow your own imagination to take over.

Chances are that you don't own a turquoise-blue platter and you haven't a hope of laying your hands on fresh orange blossoms. This doesn't mean that you shouldn't serve fried chicken until you're able to get these items. Instead, you should consider the serving pieces that you already own and decide how they can be used in place of the ones suggested here. You will find that your own creative thinking will be far more rewarding than trying to follow slavishly the specific ideas in this book.

The purpose of our suggestions is to make you feel creative and adventurous. They are intended to stimulate you to think of new ways to make your meals more meaningful and enjoyable. So do set your imagination free and try to approach the art of food presentation with your own original ideas as well as those you glean from this book.

1.
The Strategies of Food Presentation

Attitude

The concept of combining food and aesthetics is based on pleasure. Being able to please oneself, one's family, friends, and guests makes cooking a joy. The pleasure does not come only from the shopping, chopping, slicing, simmering, carving, etc. It is the sharing of the fruits of these labors that makes cooking so rewarding. If you take on more than you can comfortably handle, however, the efforts exceed the rewards and you are left with a feeling of discontent that defeats the ultimate purpose. It is better to prepare something simple than to become involved in a tedious task that is going to make you nervous or unhappy. Never allow food preparation to become a burden. Cooking should be a labor of love and a controlled effort at all times.

Helping Hands

Mealtime can be a time of warmth and sharing. Enlist help, not because you need an extra pair of hands, but because cooperative living makes everyone feel like a valuable link in the family chain. It is imperative that the duties not be haphazardly doled out. Be thoughtful when selecting chores for each person, and follow up with your guidance, instruction, and appreciation. Sharing together in the preparation of a meal is a growing experience that can bring you closer than ever before. Have your friends help too, with pleasantries such as tossing a salad or cutting a cake. Guest participation makes everyone feel at home.

The Pleasurable and Memorable Sense of Smell

Aroma is the very first stimulus we perceive at mealtime. Even before we are seated at the table a beckoning whiff of freshly brewed coffee or the haunting scent of a stockpot lazily simmering at the back of a stove can fill us with keen anticipation.

Aroma is also one of the most lasting sensations we come away with after dining. The tantalizing smells of homemade bread, cakes, and cookies, or of chestnuts roasting in the fireplace, can contribute to our fondest memories. Such captivating food fragrances create an irresistible surge of delight in all of us, and it's a wise cook who understands this.

• Before roasting a chicken, rub the cavity and skin with a freshly cut lemon for an appealing smell and flavor.

• Experiment with herbs and spices, citrus peelings, onions, and garlic to heighten cooking aromas. For example, try adding a halved, unpeeled onion to the pan when roasting meat or poultry. This will not only give off an appetizing odor but will also add flavor to the pan juices.

• Use preheated, *covered* serving bowls to present your hot foods at the table. They will not only keep your food warm but will release a cloud of heavenly aroma when the lids are raised.

• Be aware of intruding smells that might overpower the delicate nuances of your cooking. Heady perfumes, strongly scented flowers such as carnations or roses, candles with artificial fruit or lavender scents, and various fuels for table lamps should all be avoided at mealtime.

✻

Taste

Taste is perhaps the most personal of all the senses we have been endowed with. What one person likes another may dislike. Since we all have totally different capacities for taste, it's simply impossible to please everyone in the same way. There is, however, a safe approach for the cook: *season with a light hand!* This does not mean that your foods should taste bland; it means that the herbs and spices should never overpower. If you season correctly, you can use several ingredients without being able to identify a specific one. All the flavors should blend harmoniously without any one predominating. The only way to achieve such perfect balance is for the cook to taste each dish before serving. The seasoning can then be corrected by adding more, if necessary, so that the food will taste flavorful but not overwhelming or insipid. By the same token, it is imperative that only a minimal amount of salt be added to any dish. The diners will appreciate the option of adding more at table if they so choose.

Texture

Texture involves the way food feels in our mouths, and this, to a great extent, depends on the attentiveness of the cook. One of the secrets of achieving an attractive texture lies in the amount of time that food is cooked. If the person who is preparing the food happens to be thinking about something else at the time, this will invariably be detectable in the finished product, should it be overcooked. If a dry-heat method, such as baking or broiling, has been used the food may lose its moisture content and become parched and tough. If the food in a liquid preparation, such as boiling or braising, is overdone it can become soggy and fall apart. Set an alarm clock or invest in a timer with a loud ring so that you won't spoil foods by overcooking them. Vegetables, especially, benefit from a watchful eye because they can deteriorate quickly. When they are cooked to perfection, their retained vibrant color and crispy crunch are a sheer delight to the eye and the palate.

Another major secret of desirable food texture lies in the astute use of a strainer to remove stray lumps, peppercorns, garlic cloves, bay leaves, bones, seeds, and pips from various sauces, custards, gravies, juices, and soups.

Vigilant preparation is another watchword. Be sure to clean all fresh produce very carefully. Look for stray bones in fish fillets, trim off unnecessary sinew and connective tissue from meats and specialty meats such as liver, kidney, brains, etc., and thoroughly wash all salad greens to remove any sand or grit. Peel celery stalks with a vegetable peeler to remove strings and carefully check to make sure all silk has been removed before cooking corn on the cob. The improved texture justifies the extra effort in every case.

Lastly, give some thought to providing a variety of textures in every meal. A bit of chew, a little crunch, and a mite of mash are a fitting combination.

Consider these examples:

• When preparing stews and soups, stagger the addition of ingredients to the pot according to the length of time they will need to cook. Meats, onion, garlic, and tomatoes that require a lengthy simmering should be put on first. Vegetables with a more delicate heat tolerance, such as potatoes and carrots, should be added only during the final twenty to thirty minutes so that their crunchy texture is not lost through prolonged cooking. The combination of chewy but tender meat, soft potatoes, and crunchy carrots makes an interesting mélange in the mouth.

• Broiled fish fillets garnished with thin lemon slices, tender baby peas, and mashed potatoes welled with golden butter make a colorful presentation, but the dish lacks bite because all those foods are soft. To restyle the meal to include texture as well as color, you could serve the meltingly tender fish fillets with crispy golden french fries and crunchy steamed green beans flecked with pimiento butter.

• Prepare juicier hamburgers by mixing a finely shredded, small raw potato into 1 pound of ground beef.

• Improve texture by stirring:
    a diced delicious apple into potato salad;
    a coarsely chopped carrot into peanut butter;
    a few tablespoons of sesame seeds or wheat germ into your usual bread-crumb coating for fish, pork, or chicken.

These are just a few small gestures that can make a world of difference to those who will eat your food.

Color

Color is perhaps the most exciting ingredient one can use for visual impact when presenting food. Color can effectively transform everyday place settings. All that's needed is a thoughtfully selected wardrobe of accessories (cloths, place mats, runners, napkins, candles, etc.) in a variety of colors and patterns that can be mixed and matched. These can be alternated regularly to give your table a totally new look, always fresh and cheery. Naturally, table accessories should be compatible with the colors of the room where the food will be served. Vibrant red and orange accents for example can make the most of neutral grays or beige; perky pastels can offset their deep-shaded counterparts; hues of green can be worked to harmonize with violet or contrast with brilliant yellows.

There are many ways to integrate such color schemes at the table.

This is how it's done. Take a good look at the room where you eat. What color are the walls? The curtains or draperies? The upholstery on the dining chairs? The colors that you pick for the table should enhance, harmonize, or contrast with the surroundings. Your room may be a shade of pale blue, for example, hung with large, bold modern posters. Place mats, napkins, and candles might be chosen in colors that pick up the strong, vibrant colors on the walls, giving the setting a complete and total look. Perhaps the walls are covered in an intricate rose-colored floral-patterned paper and hung with delicate gold-framed landscapes. A solid, deep rose-colored cloth set off with soft green napkins that pick up the foliage in the paintings would make an attractive setting. White lace place mats could be combined with pink napkins and candles on another day. Those same pink napkins would also complement your rose-colored cloth, giving you an alternative combination. Mats and napkins in navy blue or rosy-beige tweed could be worked into the scheme to give you several choice settings.

Seasonal flowers in shades and tones that complement the table linens add elegance and warmth—pink tea roses, small pots of begonias or African violets, or a basket of rose geraniums with trailing tendrils spread over the table's surface. Add even more interest by imaginatively switching from flowers to colorful edibles—a ruffly savoy cabbage surrounded by pink emperor grapes or an arrangement of verdant bell peppers and zucchini accented with shiny eggplants and baby pink and white turnips. Such a colorful table increases dining pleasure.

Think of your plates as backgrounds and frames for your food. Keep colors and patterns, as well as size and shape, in mind when deciding which dish will be most appropriate for the food you'll be serving. The color of the plates should also be coordinated with the color scheme of the table setting. In the room described above, for example, dishes in rose, pink, white, green, or pale beige as well as plates in transparent glass or cut crystal would all look well on the table.

• Foods that lack color, such as cauliflower, mashed potatoes, poached flounder, etc., would look more appealing on colorful plates such as the pink or green ones.

• The appeal of green salads or green vegetables would be enhanced by serving them on a rosy-pink background. Consider the beauty, for example, of a lush spinach salad accented with vibrant slices of strawberries set off by a frame of rose-rimmed china.

• Dark meats such as beef or lamb, brown gravy, brightly colored vegetables in orange or yellow would benefit in appearance by a presentation on a lighter-colored background, such as oversized white or beige plates.

• Boldly colored foods, such as ripe tomatoes, red-shelled lobsters, pristine white and yellow hard-cooked egg slices, would look absolutely sensational on green plates.

The color of your plates can also reflect the mood of the day. Navel orange slices arranged in an attractive overlapping pattern on a bright yellow plate practically shout "Good morning," while curved segments of navel orange fanned on a black ceramic dish exude the drama of evening. A colorful sprig of fresh mint or a solitary strawberry placed on either dish would add a final masterful touch to show how much you care.

Colorful food is festive and appealing. From the robust red of a sweet bell pepper to the subtle beige of a mushroom, the natural colors of vegetables, herbs, and fruits can lend character and command attention to your food. When planning your menu, be attentive to the rainbow that's offered on the produce shelves. Select colorful vegetables and steam them for the minimum time to retain optimum natural color and crunch. Think color! The following suggestions may lead you to ideas of your own:

- Combine several vegetables to achieve color impact:
  Blanched carrot sticks and whole green beans
  Steamed broccoli and cauliflower flowerets
  Sliced zucchini and yellow squash
  Steamed garden peas with minced pimiento
  Corn kernels with sliced scallions
  Matchsticks of carrots, parsnips, and yellow turnips
  Sautéed broccoli flowerets and cherry tomatoes

- Add a spoonful of lemon juice to the water when cooking cauliflower to keep it snowy white.

- Line a glass bowl with ruffly outer cabbage leaves; fill the center with coleslaw and sprinkle with finely shredded raw carrot for added flavor and color appeal.

- Line a shallow wicker basket with a blue-checked linen towel; stack with two or three layers of golden corn on the cob. The cloth will keep the corn hot, as well as provide a colorful shroud.

- Serving cheese? Add a splash of color by arranging several large, freshly picked grape leaves on top of a wooden cutting board. Present a wedge of cheese on top of each leaf and garnish with small clusters of opaline grapes.

- Sliced carrots and green beans will add color to a beef stew, but the dish can be lifted to new heights if it is sprinkled with julienne strips of blanched red bell pepper and served on a bright red ceramic plate.

- Your dishes are white, but you want to serve cauliflower? Use a few leaves of raw spinach to make a colorful bed for the cooked flowerets. Sprinkle with fine threads of fresh lemon zest to enhance the aroma as well as the color.

- Pile buttered beets or sliced carrots into a large white bowl and fringe the edges with sprigs of watercress. Sprinkle with chopped chives for added flavor and contrast.

- Fluff mashed potatoes into a chocolate-brown bowl. Even though you've already seasoned them, allow an additional pat of golden butter to melt in a center well.

- Enliven a potato salad by studding it with color. Unpeeled, chopped red apple and sliced scallions will appeal to the palate as well as the eye. Serve it on a Boston lettuce leaf.

• Fan three grapefruit segments on a shiny blue plate and place three overlapping slices of kiwi at the base of the fan. Lightly sprinkle the grapefruit with freshly minced parsley.

• Invert an individual can of tuna into the hollow of a red cabbage leaf that has been placed on a green plate. Top the tuna with a spoonful of mayonnaise and tiny capers; garnish with a hard-cooked egg half and two black olives.

• Canned vegetables can quickly be turned into a colorful layered salad when unexpected guests arrive. Separately toss the vegetables in salad dressing, then arrange them in individual layers in a clear glass bowl. Sliced carrots, whole button mushrooms, asparagus tips, red kidney beans, and whole green beans make an interesting and flavorful combination.

• Eye-catching foods can be placed in clear glass bowls. Try a mixture of quartered radishes, sliced celery, whole black olives, crumbled feta cheese, and chopped parsley.

• Who could resist the simplicity of a sunny-side egg in the company of two asparagus spears on a golden-yellow plate?

The Cook's Color Chart

Nature provides us with a rainbow of colors to eat. The following chart is like an artist's palette that can be used to dress and garnish your foods so that they will look more appealing.

GREEN VEGETABLES

Artichokes
Arugula
Asparagus
Bok choy
Broad beans
Broccoli
Brussels sprouts
Cabbage
Celery
Cucumber peel

Dandelion greens
Fennel stalks
Gherkins
Green beans
Green bell peppers
Green chili peppers
Kale
Kohlrabi
Leeks
Lettuces:
  Bibb
  Boston
  Chicory
  Escarole
  Iceberg
  Romaine
Okra
Olives
Peas
Pickles
Scallions
Snow peas
Sorrel
Spinach
Watercress
Zucchini peel

Fresh Herbs:
Basil
Chervil
Chives
Dill
Mint
Parsley

Fruits
Avocados
Grapes
Green apples
Greengage plums
Lime zest
Kiwi fruit
Pears

Other
Pistachio nuts (shelled)

BLUE/PURPLE VEGETABLES
Eggplant
Red cabbage
Turnip parings

Fruits
Blueberries
Grapes
Plums

RED VEGETABLES
Beets
Bell peppers
Chili peppers
Kidney beans
Pimientos
Radishes
Red cabbage
Red leaf lettuce
Red onions
Red potatoes (unpeeled)

Fruits
 Apples
 Cherries
 Cranberries
 Pomegranate
  seeds
 Raspberries
 Red currants
 Strawberries
 Tomatoes
 Watermelon

Other
 Lumpfish caviar

BLACK VEGETABLES
 Olives
 Truffles

Fruits
 Blackberries
 Black currants
 Elderberries
 Prunes

Other
 Caviar

BROWN/BEIGE VEGETABLES
 Mushrooms
 Potatoes (unpeeled)

Fruits
 Dates

 Figs (dried)
 Raisins

Other
 Almonds
 Anchovies
 Croutons
 Pecans
 Walnuts

ORANGE/YELLOW VEGETABLES
 Bell peppers
 Carrots
 Chili peppers
 Corn kernels
 Pumpkin
 Rutabaga
 Squash
 Sweet potatoes
 Wax beans
 Yams

Fruits
 Apples
 Apricots
 Cantaloupes
 Grapefruit zest
 Kumquats
 Lemon zest
 Loquats
 Mangoes
 Nectarines
 Oranges
 Orange zest
 Papayas
 Peaches

Persimmons
Pineapple
Tangerines
Tangerine zest

Other
Egg yolks
Golden caviar

WHITE VEGETABLES
Belgian endive
Bean sprouts
Cauliflower
Celeriac
Cucumber (peeled)
Daikon (Japanese radish)
Enok mushrooms
Fennel bulb
Great Northern beans
Hearts of palm
Leeks (white part)
Lima beans (dried)
Mushrooms (cultivated)
Onions

Parsnips
Potatoes (peeled)
Scallions (white only)
Summer squash (peeled)
Turnips
Zucchini (peeled)

Fruits
Apples (peeled)
Bananas (peeled)
Grapefruit segments
Honeydew melon
Lychees
Pears (peeled)
White currants

Other
Brazil nuts (shelled)
Cashews
Coconut (grated)
Egg white

Lighting

Choice of lighting contributes greatly to the style and atmosphere one wishes to create at mealtime. Here, too, variety can add interest to your table, and it is important to change your form of lighting from time to time.

The magic of candlelight involves moving shadows. It creates a festive aura for holiday entertaining and it holds back the gloom of cold winter nights. It can also make complexions sparkle, as well as illuminate crystal and glass. It's soft, warm, sometimes romantic, but always inviting. Search for imaginative ways to hold the alluring glow of candlelight.

Candles and candleholders in assorted shapes, colors, and sizes are enchanting accents at any table:

• Arrange four small pots of African violets in the center of your table. Set three dark pink and two light pink candles in low candlesticks and place them around and in between the plants. Fill in the gaps with shiny eggplants and purple bows.

• Set a bushy Swedish ivy plant in the center of your table and push six to eight tall, thin taper candles into the soil. Blow the candles out when and if the flames get too close to the foliage.

• Place three large glass hurricane shades down the center of your table. Fill them about a quarter of the way up with a mixture of fresh cranberries and unshelled almonds. Insert a purple 12-inch candle in the center of each shade.

• Select a half dozen small bell peppers that will stand steady and straight. Hollow out the stem end of each pepper. Place a glass votive candleholder with candle inside each pepper. Arrange these on your table as part of a vegetable centerpiece containing summer squash, cucumbers, cauliflower, and carrots.

• Hollow the stem ends of several red and green apples just enough to encase small votive candles. Make sure the apples stand steady. Place a fruit basket of uncut apples in the center of your table and surround it with the apple candleholders.

• Select any 8-ounce can of fruit or vegetables from your cupboard. Use the can as a base to hold a fat (3-inch-diameter), tall (8-inch-high) candle. Trim the bottoms off a bunch of celery, for example, so that the

stalks measure about 6 inches in length. Tie these upright around the candle-topped can with a colorful ribbon.

• Set 3-inch votive candles inside large balloon wineglasses. Fill each glass with ½ inch of water and float fresh violet blossoms or other tiny flowers on the water's surface.

• Souvenir wine bottles from special celebrations such as birthdays or weddings make attractive as well as sentimental candleholders on the following anniversary.

• Vary the placement of candles on the dining table—spread them around the table or cluster them in one or more groups.

• No one can dispute the beauty of candlelight, but when used as the only source of light at mealtime it may be insufficient. For best results, experiment with combinations of candlelight and low lighting from another source.

• Install a rheostat or dimmer on the light switch in the room where you eat, so that your lighting can fluctuate with your moods. The lowered light combines well with candlelight.

• Oil lamps can be attractive, but be aware that many fuels emit a scent that will clash with food. Artificially scented candles such as lavender or sandalwood would also be intrusive at mealtime. Shop for unscented fuels and candles, if they are to be used at the table.

• Pink light bulbs in your lighting fixtures will give off a warm rosy glow.

• If you have a working fireplace, use it from time to time. Even if the fireplace is in another room, it will put everyone in a comfortable frame of mind. If you have a fireplace that can't be lit or you'd rather not go to the trouble, buy one or two dozen large, fat candles in various lengths and arrange them inside the fire pit. If desired, the candles can be surrounded with freshly cut branches of greenery. This makes a very effective lighting arrangement.

• Outdoor lighting for alfresco dining requires special consideration in order to keep unwanted insects under control. Blue lights attract bugs, so they should be avoided, but yellow lights are reputed to keep mosquitoes away. Yellow bug bulbs are usually available at hardware stores and sometimes at the supermarket. There are also special light fixtures that electrocute insects, but these are relatively expensive.

• Patio lights and torches are another fine way to control insects while achieving a dramatic lighting effect at the same time. Kerosene or some other insect repellent fuel may be burned in these.

• Citronella candles can create a romantic atmosphere while serving the dual purpose of repelling insects at an outdoor meal. They do give off a distinct odor, but it is not unbearable.

• Use attractive hurricane shades to protect candles from the wind when dining outdoors.

2.
Kitchen Equipment

As the popularity of gourmet cooking increases, more and more people are gradually becoming aware of the dazzling array of implements available for use in the kitchen. It seems as if some sort of gadget, tool, pan, or machine has been invented for every conceivable task. While many of these are practical items, others are mere novelties. Deciding whether a piece of equipment is essential or frivolous depends on how much use you will get out of it. But even trivial utensils can be worth their while if they are fun to use and contribute to your enjoyment in the kitchen. Many of the gadgets, such as the strawberry huller, can even be wielded by children, enabling them to accomplish tasks that would otherwise be too difficult.

Without doubt a wardrobe of good-quality, high-carbon, stainless steel cutlery is one of the most important parts of any home kitchen. Few other implements can perform as many tasks as a set of sharp blades. With only a well-balanced chef's knife, several paring knives, and a swivel-action vegetable peeler one can chop, mince, dice, or slice all kinds of raw or cooked foods into interesting, colorful shapes. Specialized accessories, such as the following gadgets, knives, decorative molds, and pans, can increase your pleasure and creative ability in the kitchen and make it even simpler to add artistry to the food you serve.

❋

Gadgets and Tools

APPLE CORER   Anyone who has ever tried to hollow out the center of an apple knows how difficult it can be. The neatest way to accomplish this chore is with the tool designed solely for that purpose. It has a 4-inch wooden or plastic handle attached to a 4-inch trough-shaped stainless steel blade. One model has a serrated cutting edge while another has a sharp metal cutting ring at the tip of the blade. To use, stand an apple on a cutting board. Hold it firmly in one hand while inserting the corer into the stem end. Push straight down and rotate the corer as you force it through to the other end of the apple. Retract the tool to remove the core. It may be necessary to repeat the procedure if all the center bits do not come out on the first attempt.

• Fill the apple cavity with a sausage stuffing mixture and bake in a moderate oven, 350° F., until tender, about 1 hour. Serve as a colorful, aromatic, and tasty accompaniment to roasted poultry and game birds. Surround a platter holding the roasted fowl with the stuffed baked apples. Arrange individual portions of cooked whole green beans in between the apples.

• Fill the apple cavity with a brown sugar, cinnamon, and butter mixture and bake in a moderate oven, 350° F., until tender. Use to surround a roasted pork loin or fresh ham. Arrange steamed broccoli flowerets in between the apples.

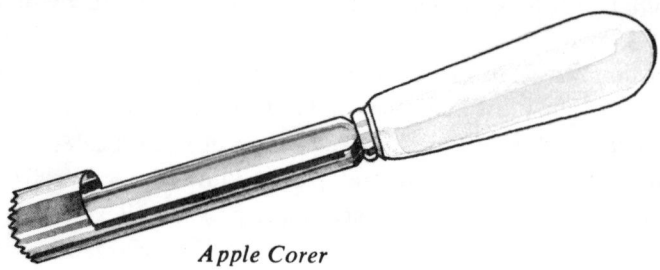

Apple Corer

APPLE AND PEAR DIVIDER   This sturdy metal device cores and sections the fruit in one swift downward motion. The center space for the core is a ¾-inch ring with sharp stainless steel blades radiating toward the circular frame, which is 4 inches in diameter. Two metal handles positioned on the frame allow for a firm grip.

• To retain the snow-white color of freshly cut apples and pears, sprinkle them with lemon juice or soak in a mixture of lemon juice or ascorbic acid and water, allowing about 1 teaspoon of juice or ascorbic acid to 1 cup of water.

• Fan wedges of unpeeled red apples and green pears around a generous slice of Brie or Camembert cheese.

Apple and Pear Divider

• For a colorful luncheon dish, position a mound of chicken salad in the center of a plate. Surround the salad with a wreath of watercress, tucking the stem ends under the mound. Alternate wedges of unpeeled red apple and yellow pear peeping out from under the watercress.

• For breakfast or a snack, turn a cupful of honey-flavored yogurt into a crystal compote dish. Sprinkle with wheat germ. Place the dish on a large plate and surround with wedges of unpeeled apple and pear to be used in place of a spoon for eating the yogurt.

ASPIC, GARNISHING, AND TRUFFLE CUTTERS These resemble miniature metal cookie cutters. The tiny shapes usually range from ¼ inch to ½ inch, ¾ inch, and 1 inch in diameter and are sold in sets of a dozen designs or more. They generally take the form of spades, diamonds, hearts, clubs, crescents, leaves, animals, stars, or flowers, just to name a few. Use them to cut these fancy shapes out of aspic/gelatin, truffles, or thin slices of raw or cooked vegetables such as beets, carrots, turnips, radishes, or squash. They can also punch designs out of pickles, pimientos, olives, hard-cooked egg whites, or blanched peppers. Use the cutouts to ornament cold salads and platters, canapés and hors d'oeuvre, open-faced sandwiches, or clear soups. Cut small designs out of pastry scraps and use them to decorate your pies or meats en croûte.

• Border a solid-color platter with delicate petal-thin vegetable cutouts. Slice carrots, parsnips, beets, and rutabaga as thinly as possible. Cut the thin slices into interesting shapes, using the aspic cutters or a sharp knife. Thin slices of red-ringed radishes may be cut in half and used in the design. Feathery dill snippets can be used for greenery. Use the decorated platter to present scrambled eggs for a crowd, a whole baked fish, or a roasted bird or piece of meat.

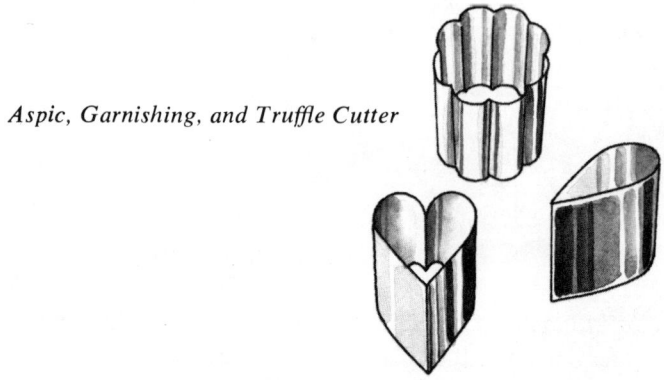

Aspic, Garnishing, and Truffle Cutter

• Cook one or two whole peeled carrots in clear consommé about an hour before serving. When the carrots are tender, remove them, cool, and slice into ⅛-inch coins. Cut into flower shapes and use to garnish the clear soup.

Should you find these fancy aspic cutters too expensive, it is not difficult to make your own stylized versions. Use the metal tops from some discarded lipstick tubes. With a pair of pliers, reshape the open end of the tube into decorative designs: ovals, squares, hearts, and so forth.

Kitchen Equipment 19

Wash them well and sterilize them in boiling water before use. For especially tiny cutters, apply the same make-your-own technique to pens and pencils that have eraser tips. Remove the eraser and then reshape the eraser container or use it as is to cut out minute circle shapes. If the cut-out designs should get stuck inside your homemade cutters, they can easily be removed with a needle or straight pin.

BIRD'S-NEST MAKER This invention transforms shredded raw potatoes, carrots, yams, or turnips into crunchy containers that can be filled with colorful vegetables such as peas, diced carrots, or corn kernels studded with pimiento. Lightly sauced stews, curries, seafood, and creamed foods also make delightful fillings. Thin noodles that have been precooked in sweetened milk can be fried into crispy dessert cups for poached fruit, ice cream, or puddings. Thinly sliced soft bread can be converted into a breakfast nest for poached or scrambled eggs.

Birds-Nest Maker

The apparatus consists of two wire baskets, about 3 inches and 4 inches in diameter, each attached to a 13-inch metal handle. The smaller basket fits inside the larger basket and they are held in place by a metal clamp that slides on the handles. Line the larger basket with shredded food and insert the smaller basket to keep the food in place. Slide the metal clamp so that the baskets remain in position. The nests are then deep-fried in bubbling oil. Detailed instructions are included.

BOUQUET GARNI BAGS These dainty washable cotton sacks are just what the doctor ordered for the cook who forgets to remove bay leaves, peppercorns, garlic cloves, etc., from sauces, soups, and stews. Fill the pouch, which measures about 2½ × 3½ inches, with the various herbs and spices required in your recipe, tie the drawstring, and immerse in the cooking pot. Remove the bag before serving. The used herbs can be discarded and the bag washed for reuse. Homemade bouquet garni bags can be fashioned by wrapping the herbs and spices in clean cheesecloth squares and securing the bundle with cotton thread. Note: see Wonderball.

BUTTER CURLERS There's nothing more refreshing than serving an everyday food that we take for granted in a very special way. Such is the effect when enchanting sculptured butter curls are placed on the table instead of the usual block or tub. Mastering this tool takes a bit of practice, but it's not difficult and the results are pleasing. Butter curlers measure about 7 inches long, including a wooden or plastic handle. The apparatus is available in several equally effective shapes, such as a hook, a rake, or a claw scoop. All have sharp serrated edges. Simply scrape the teeth across a chilled stick of butter and pull off a golden curl. Place curls in a bowl of crushed ice to prevent them from melting out of shape. A sculptured melon-ball cutter can double as a tool for this purpose.

BUTTER PADDLES Make irresistible butter balls with a textured crisscross surface. Wooden butter paddles are usually made from birchwood because it doesn't absorb butterfat readily. The paddles are ingrained with deep ridges to impart their design. Place a dollop of cold butter at the end of one paddle and, holding a paddle in each hand, rub them together in a circular pattern. Place the balls in a bowl of crushed ice to prevent them from melting out of shape.

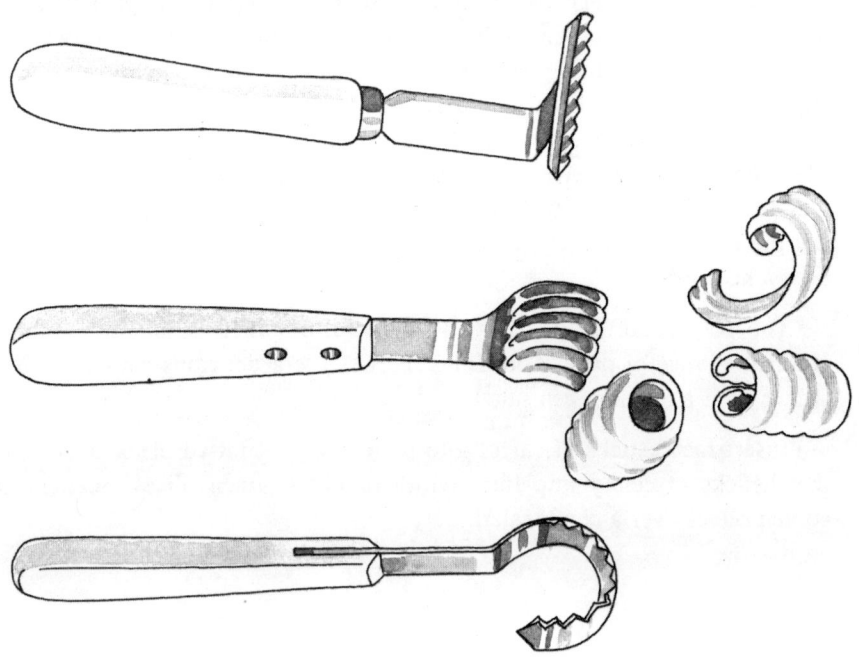

Butter Curlers (top)

Butter Paddles (bottom)

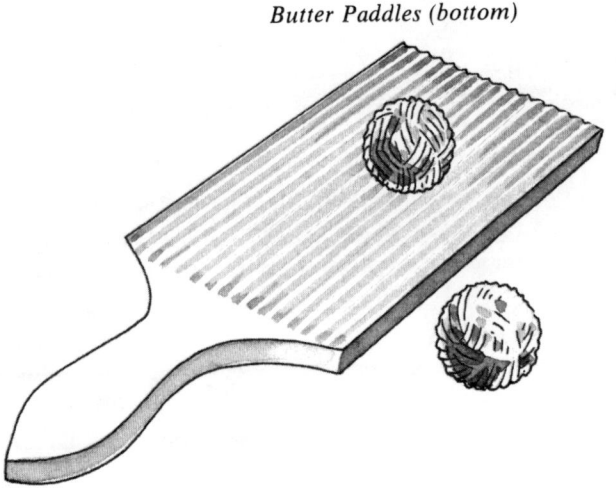

CHERRY AND OLIVE PITTER Eating is twice the pleasure when you don't have to worry about chipping a tooth. This relatively inexpensive tool makes fun of a normally tedious job and is one that your children might enjoy using. There are various models, but they all operate like a paper punch. Unfasten the catch which secures the handles when not in use. Place one cherry or olive in the cup or socket and squeeze the two handles together. The action forces a cutting rod through the fruit and pokes out the pit. Unfortunately, it pits only one piece of fruit at a time. But it does a neat job.

• Top cold breakfast cereal with a handful of pitted Bing cherries for a colorful change of pace. Too, Bing cherries are a delicious curiosity when strewn over a tossed green salad.

• Insert matchsticks of carrot into the cavities of pitted black olives and matchsticks of celery into the cavities of pitted green olives. Scatter the stuffed olives over a chef's salad.

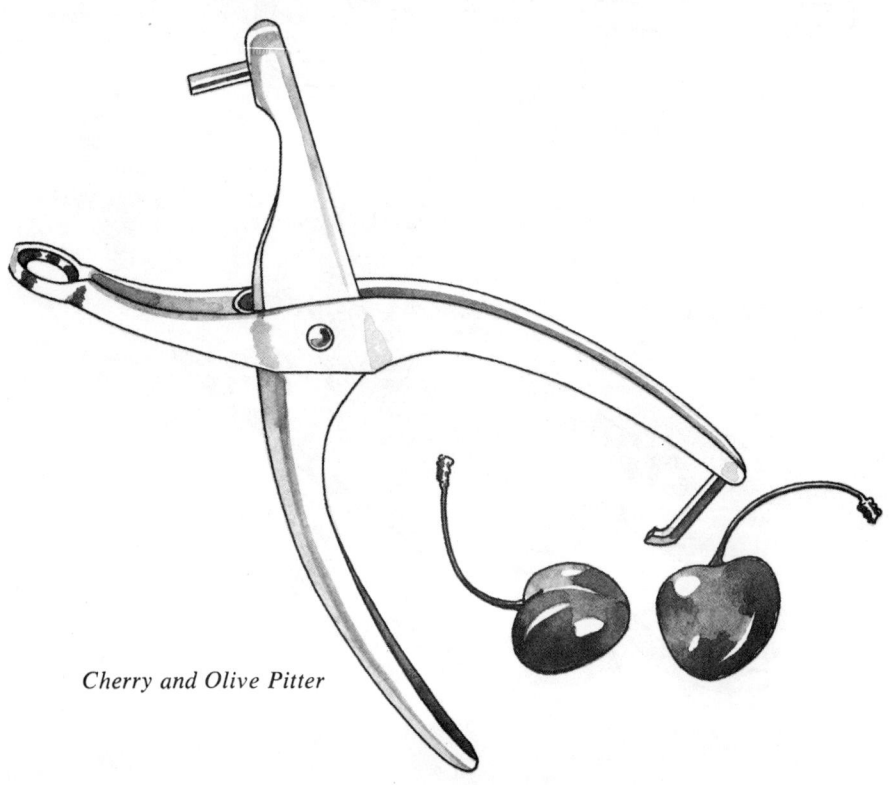

Cherry and Olive Pitter

CITRUS SCORER AND STRIPPER   This is a useful dual-purpose tool. It produces thin strips of citrus peel such as lemon twists, which can be candied or used to garnish coffee or cocktails. The resulting scored fruit may then be sliced into decorative rounds which can be used to enhance tea, punches, spiced or long drinks, soups, or seafood, just to name a few. The tool is approximately 6 inches long, including a plastic or wooden handle. The tip is shaped into a flat, round stainless steel head with a hole bored in it. The far side of the hole has a sharpened lip which serves as the cutting edge. The angle of the blade is perfect for round, thick-skinned fruit, but the tool can also be used to score radishes or flute mushrooms.

CITRUS SHELLER   This is a simple flat cutting tool made for hollowing out all kinds of citrus fruits. It resembles a metal ski, just over 5 inches in length, and has a sharp cutting edge on the underside. Draw a line around the circumference of a citrus fruit. Using the cutting edge of the peeler, carve out a thin strip of skin along the guideline. Insert the slightly curved end of the tool between the peel and the fruit and gently maneuver it around until the pulp is loosened. Hold the fruit in both hands and twist the halves in opposite directions. You will then be left holding two perfectly shaped citrus cups that can be filled with marmalade, jam, ice cream, sherbet, fruit salad, cold soufflé, or whatever else comes to mind. The peeled fruit might need to be divested of its white pith, but it can then be sectioned and used in a variety of ways, or you might wish to halve the fruit and squeeze out the juice.

• Fill hollowed orange halves with mashed sweet potatoes and arrange around a platter of baked ham.

• Hollowed lime shells make colorful containers for individual portions of raisins at a children's party or snack time.

• Prepare your choice of fruit-flavored gelatin according to package directions. Ladle lukewarm gelatin mixture into hollowed citrus shells and chill until set. To prevent the rounded shells from tipping, set them in muffin pans or on top of miniature wreaths made of crushed aluminum foil which have been placed on a tray or baking sheet. When the gelatin is firm, cut the citrus shells in half to form colorful gelatin wedges. Arrange the wedges as an edible garnish around a roast turkey or on a plate of cottage cheese and fruit. Select gelatin colors that will contrast with the rind of the shells to be filled, such as raspberry gelatin in grapefruit shells, pineapple gelatin in orange shells, lime gelatin in lemon shells, or blackberry gelatin in lime shells.

• Bed a roast duckling on a colorful and aromatic blanket of blanched julienne orange strips. Scrape out the white pith from about 8 or 10 hollowed orange shells. Cut the rind into julienne strips. Blanch strips in a pan of boiling water for 3 minutes, drain, and pat dry with paper towels. Arrange strips on a serving platter and top with quartered roast duckling portions.

CITRUS ZESTER   Zest is the colored skin of citrus fruit, and it contains all the flavorful oils. The white pith underneath the rind is bitter and undesirable. Normally one would use a grater when tiny shavings of citrus zest are called for. But graters are impractical for this purpose because they remove the pith as well as the rind. A zester is a tool that scrapes off only the outer skin of the citrus fruit, producing threadlike strands of colorful zest that can be used as is or chopped to a finer texture. The tool is approximately 6 inches in length with a plastic or wooden handle. The cutting end is made of stainless steel and has five tiny, very sharp holes. The tool can also be used for decorating sticks of butter or for scoring carrots, squash, or cucumbers before they are sliced into rounds.

• Garnish a thin lemon slice with curly shreds of orange or lime zest. Set the garnished slice adrift in a bowl of black bean soup.

• Sprinkle cucumber spears with threads of lemon zest. Serve them on a blue plate holding a small crystal cup of avocado dip.

EGG RINGS   To make perfectly round fried eggs, place these buttered rings in a hot buttered pan or skillet and break the eggs directly into the rings. Each metal corral can hold one or two eggs and some models have heat-resistant wooden handles. To make your own egg rings, simply remove the tops and bottoms from tuna cans and sterilize the rings in boiling water. Handle these with care in case any sharp edges have been gouged out by the can opener. Use a folded piece of wax paper to protect your fingers when buttering the rings before use.

• Place a perfectly round fried egg between the slices of a toasted and buttered whole wheat English muffin to make a delicious and pretty breakfast or snack sandwich.

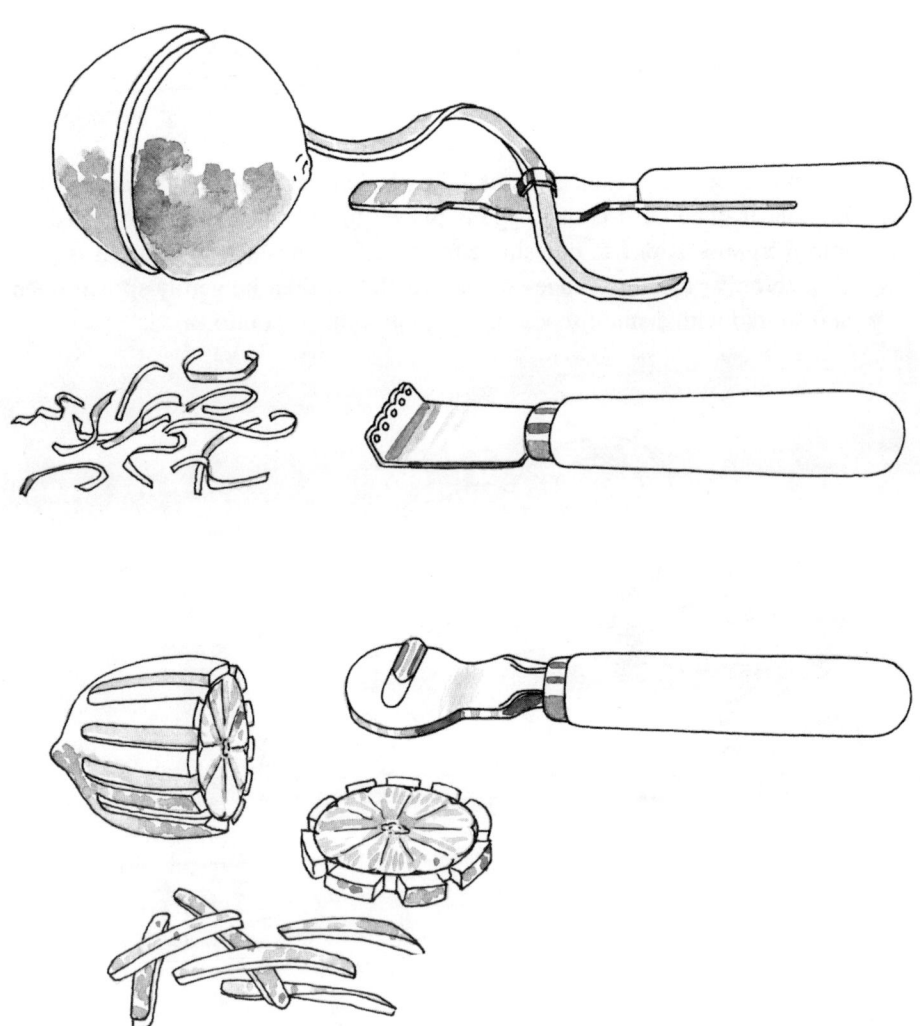

Citrus Zester

EGG SLICER Obvious in its function, this gadget makes short work of slicing or chopping hard-cooked eggs. The slicer has stainless steel wires set into a cast aluminum frame. The body has a double oval depression so that an egg can be sliced either lengthwise or crosswise, or both to make uniform cubes. Great for garnishing soups, salads, and sandwiches. The tool is approximately 8 inches long with half its length taken up by double handles.

EGG WEDGER This tool is about 7 inches long and vaguely resembles the Egg Slicer. The hard-cooked egg is placed upright in the cup and wedged into 6 equal sections in one single motion. For an unusual effect, it is possible to only partially wedge an egg, which can then be gently spread open and stuffed with a small scoop of tuna, chicken, or potato salad.

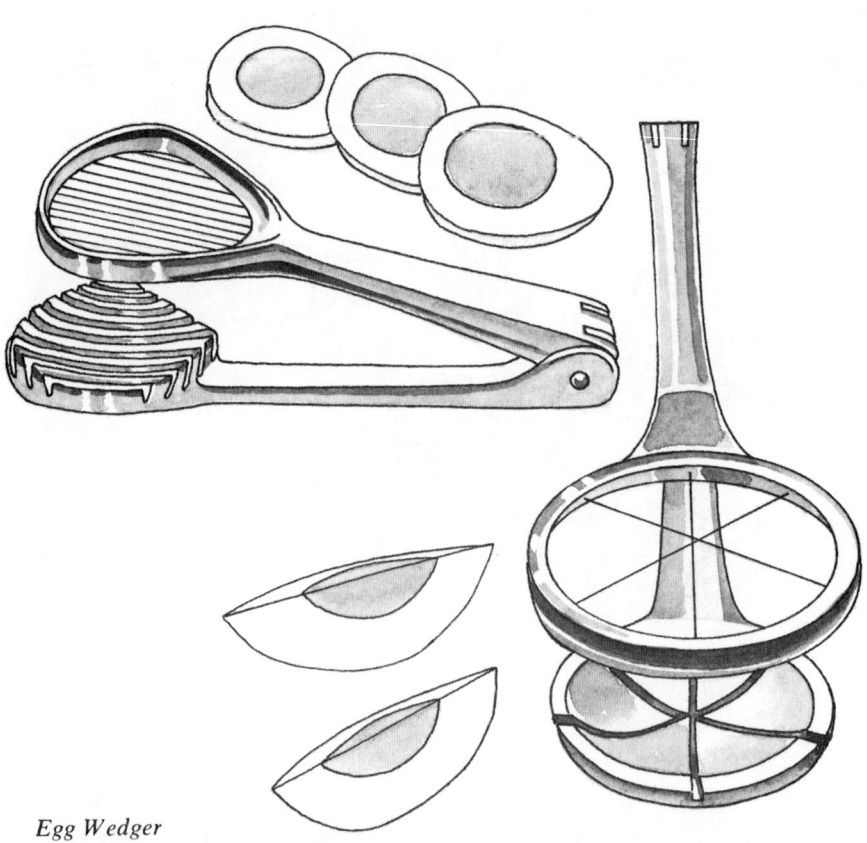

Egg Wedger

GRATERS   These nifty gadgets come in an assortment of shapes and sizes, and most kitchens are equipped with a manual or electric model, or both. The object is to find one that is handy, efficient, uncomplicated, and easy to clean. Hand-held rotary types with multitextured changeable cylinders or table-model cheese graters can really enliven an otherwise ordinary meal. You can serve freshly grated cheese more often. Sprinkle it on eggs, a variety of buttered vegetables, and noodles as well as Italian and other ethnic specialties. Some models are also suitable for grating hard chocolate which can be sprinkled over whipped cream.

Graters

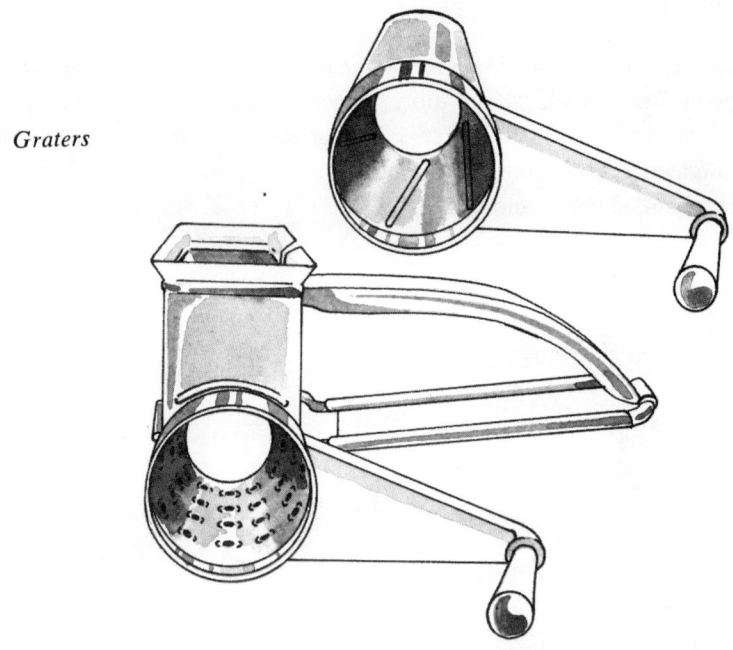

GRINDERS AND MILLS   Table models for grinding peppercorns are not unusual. However, you can add a bit of interest here by placing two on the table—one in a dark-stained wood for spicier black peppercorns and one in a light or natural wood finish for milder white peppercorns. A salt mill for grinding rock salt and a nutmeg grinder are other charming offerings for the table. A light dusting of nutmeg will give a surprise lift to spinach, Swiss chard, brussels sprouts, baked acorn squash, and poached fruits, to name just a few uses.

28   WOMAN'S DAY *Serving Food with Style*

HONEY DIPPER   Serve honey instead of sugar or jam at the table for a delightfully different and nutritious treat at breakfast, snack, or dessert time. Remove the dipper from a jar of honey and swirl it around a bit. Because the dipper is shaped like a small beehive on a stick, the honey remains in the hollowed-out crevices instead of dripping all over the table. If you have an attractive honey jar, all the better. If not, soaking the label off a store-bought jar will make it more appealing.

• Honey that is very thick will be easier to handle if it is slightly warmed prior to serving. Place the jar in a pan of hot water for about 2 minutes before bringing it to the table. The heat will thin the texture somewhat.

ICE CREAM SCOOPS   Serving ice cream can be accomplished with a large spoon, but it looks much more delectable when it's shaped with its own device. Scoops are available in a variety of sizes and shapes including round, oval, and conical. Use a larger scoop to make perfect spheres of ice cream, sherbet, and cottage cheese.

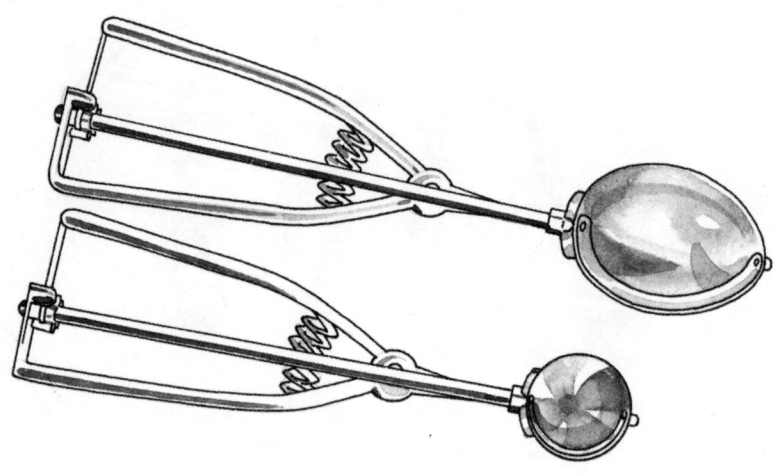

Ice Cream Scoops

• Serve a perfect scoop of butter on a wooden board with a round loaf of fresh-baked whole wheat bread.

• Use the scoop to shape individual mounds of rice or mashed potatoes and arrange them around a platter of curry or stew. Separate the mounds with colorful bunches of steamed carrot sticks and whole green beans.

• For light lunch, serve a scoop of cottage cheese in the cavity of a papaya half. Stud the cheese with pineapple chunks and seedless green grapes.

• On a sweltering hot day, dive into a mound of green watercress topped with a scoop of frosty tomato sherbet.

• Coconut ice cream welled in a cantaloupe half or lemon sherbet in the cavity of an avocado can each be sprinkled with shredded coconut for a stimulating presentation.

Smaller scoops are perfect for combining clouds of ice cream or sherbet with colorful fruits in a crystal bowl, for example, puffs of peach and vanilla ice cream islanded in a pond of raspberries. The small scoops can also be used for shaping melon, meat, or butter balls. Or use the small scoops to present two or more flavor or color combinations in one serving, such as nuggetlike scoops of lemon and raspberry sherbet with scoops of ricotta cheese surrounded by a minute puddle of glistening chocolate sauce.

• Slightly soften ice creams and sherbets before serving by allowing them to stand at room temperature for about 10 minutes. If the frozen confections are too cold, they can deaden the taste buds.

❋

LEMON WEDGE BAGS It seems very elegant to dress lemon wedges in washable cotton net panties with an elastic edge. These amusing frivolities prevent the juice from squirting out of bounds while at the same time imprisoning the seeds. Use them when serving tea, raw, poached, or broiled seafood, or wedges of ripe melon.

MEAT FRILLS Add a crowning touch to drumsticks or exposed chop bones with fringed paper frills. Homemade versions are the most beautiful and unpretentious. Cut plain white or decorative paper into 4 × 4-inch squares and fold in half. Using scissors, cut a thin fringe across the folded edge of the paper about a third to a half the way through. Loosely wrap the uncut end of the folded paper square around the drumstick or chop bone to determine its size. Secure with cellophane tape. Place the frills on the meat before serving.

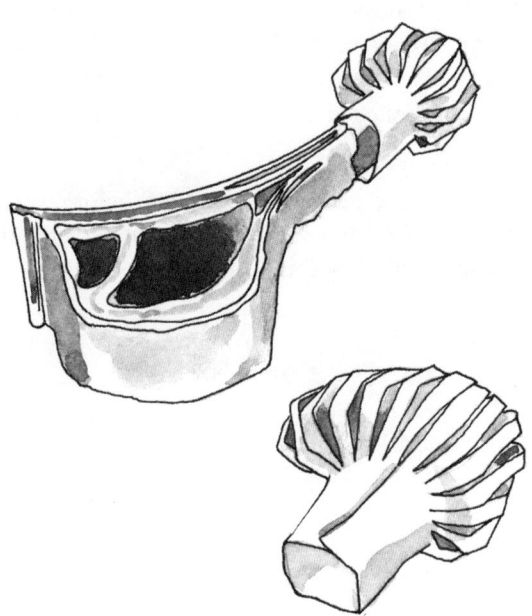

MELON-BALL CUTTERS These tools come in a variety of sizes ranging from 1¼ inches in diameter to ⅛ inch and are used to make fanciful spheres, ovals, or scalloped food carvings. Each tool is approximately 7 inches long, including a wooden or plastic handle. A stainless-steel cup is attached at either or one end. To use, press the metal cup into the food and rotate the instrument to dig out the carved orbs. The exciting news is that the use of these cutters is not restricted solely to carving melon. Balls can also be shaped out of cheese, butter, gelatin, jellied cranberry sauce, and any firm-fleshed fruits or vegetables.

• Use the tool to hollow the centers of cherry tomatoes. Stuff the cavities with cheese, steak tartare, or chicken, tuna, potato, or egg salad. Top with chopped chives or parsley and use as an hors d'oeuvre or to garnish cold meat or salad platters.

• Scoop out the centers of large fresh mushrooms with a melon-ball cutter. Sauté briefly and fill cavities with petits pois. Use to surround a meat loaf or grilled flank steak.

• Carve small spheres out of carrots, potatoes, turnips, or rutabagas. Sauté in clarified butter until tender. Present as an accompaniment to roast poultry or pork.

• Use a zigzag knife to cut a cantaloupe in half. Scoop out the seeds. Use a scalloped melon baller and a pea-sized melon baller to carve out one half of the cut melon. Combine the carved melon balls with a few seedless green grapes and pile the mixture into the cavity of the remaining melon half. Top with a sprig of bright green mint.

MUSHROOM BRUSH   The texture of raw mushrooms is as delicate as the flavor, and therefore proper cleaning is an important consideration. If washed in water, their natural qualities can easily be destroyed because mushrooms act very much like a dry sponge soaking up liquid. A small, nylon-bristled mushroom brush seems to be the most practical way of accomplishing this task. It resembles a tiny scrub brush approximately 2 inches wide and 4 inches long. Slightly dampen the soft bristles with lemon juice, which will prevent the mushrooms from turning brown, and gently brush away any clinging particles of dirt. Rinse, shake out, and redampen the brush with lemon juice before each use.

• Float a solitary thin slice of raw mushroom as a garnish atop a bowl of tomato soup.

• Cut a raw mushroom into thin slices. Discard the round ends by using them in a salad, soup, or stew. Arrange the thin slices in overlapping layers on top of an omelet.

• Chill a solid-color serving dish or platter in the refrigerator. Using a tweezer, dip thinly sliced mushrooms into a bowl of liquid beef or chicken aspic, and arrange the mushrooms side by side around the edge of the plate to form a decorative border. Chill until the aspic-coated mushrooms are set in place. Use the plate to serve a mound of fresh spinach salad or a piping-hot tangle of spaghetti topped with mushroom sauce.

MUSHROOM FLUTER   This tool resembles the citrus stripper except that the cutting edge is located at the tip rather than on the side of the metal head. It is used to score raw mushroom caps in a radiating pinwheel design. The mushrooms must be very fresh and firm so that they don't break or tear under the pressure of being carved. Position the cutting edge of the fluter at the center of a raw mushroom cap and gently pull the device down toward the edge of the mushroom. Slightly turn the mushroom cap as you cut so that the carved ridge is shaped in a spiral. Repeat this movement around the mushroom at about ½-inch spaced intervals. The fluter may also be used to score radishes from top to bottom.

• Gently dab scored raw mushroom caps with lemon juice to prevent them from turning brown.

• Use scored mushroom caps and scored radishes as raw vegetable dippers on a platter of crudités.

• Lightly oil 6 demitasse cups and pour a thin layer of liquid aspic into the bottom of each. Chill until set. Place a fluted mushroom, cap down, on the set layer of aspic. Spoon a little more liquid aspic into the cup and chill to set the mushroom in place. Finally, spoon in enough liquid aspic to cover the mushroom completely and chill until set. Unmold the aspic mushrooms and use to garnish a platter of cold sliced roast beef or turkey.

• Gently sauté scored mushroom caps in butter. Use 2 or 3 per serving as an accompaniment to sliced steak.

• Serve a sautéed boneless breast of chicken in a cream sauce and top with a sautéed scored mushroom cap. Tuck a few leaves of watercress or parsley under the cap for added color.

• Flute caps prior to making mushrooms à la Grecque or marinated mushrooms. Serve them on a bed of curly chicory as an appetizer or appoint them as a garnish for salad platters.

PASTRY BAGS   Cone-shaped bags made of nylon, plastic-lined, or canvas fabrics are used with an assortment of decorative metal nozzles. A plastic coupler is dropped into the bag and a selected nozzle is screwed onto the coupler. This enables the tip to be changed without emptying the bag of its contents. Once assembled, the bag can be filled with frosting, whipped cream, mashed potatoes, or other foods of pliable consistency and be squeezed out into various designs, depending on the shape and size of the fitted tip. Some have jagged ridges for making stars and flowers; some are specially forged for molding petals and leaves; while others are flattened to produce a ribbon effect. Practice in piping out decorative patterns can be done on a clean plate or baking sheet. The decorations can then be scraped up with a spatula and put back into the bag for reuse. Aside from

A centerpiece as simple as two floating carnations and a single candle can add elegance to a table setting.

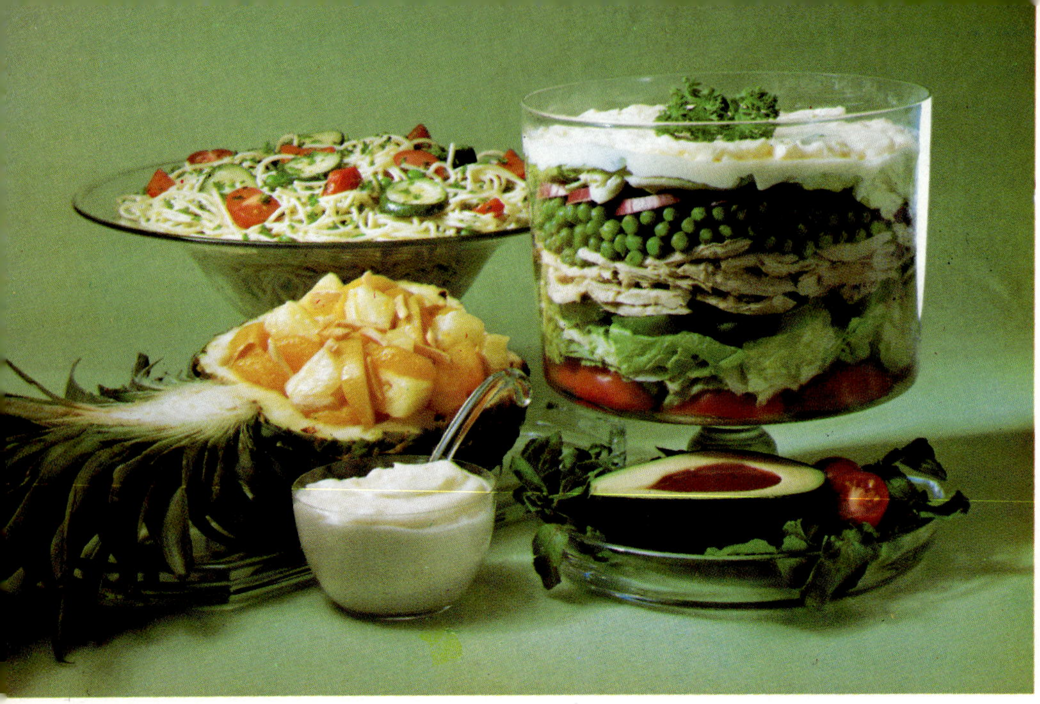

IRWIN HOROWITZ

Festive salads contribute color as well as nutrition to a well-planned meal. An avocado or pineapple salad can be presented in the shell that nature has provided; cold spaghetti becomes glamorous when tossed with colorful vegetables; cold meat and vegetables acquire new elegance when layered in a glass bowl.

Garnishes should complement but not overpower any dish. Simple garnishes, such as mint sprigs, whole strawberries, and lemon slices draw attention to food without causing a flamboyant distraction.

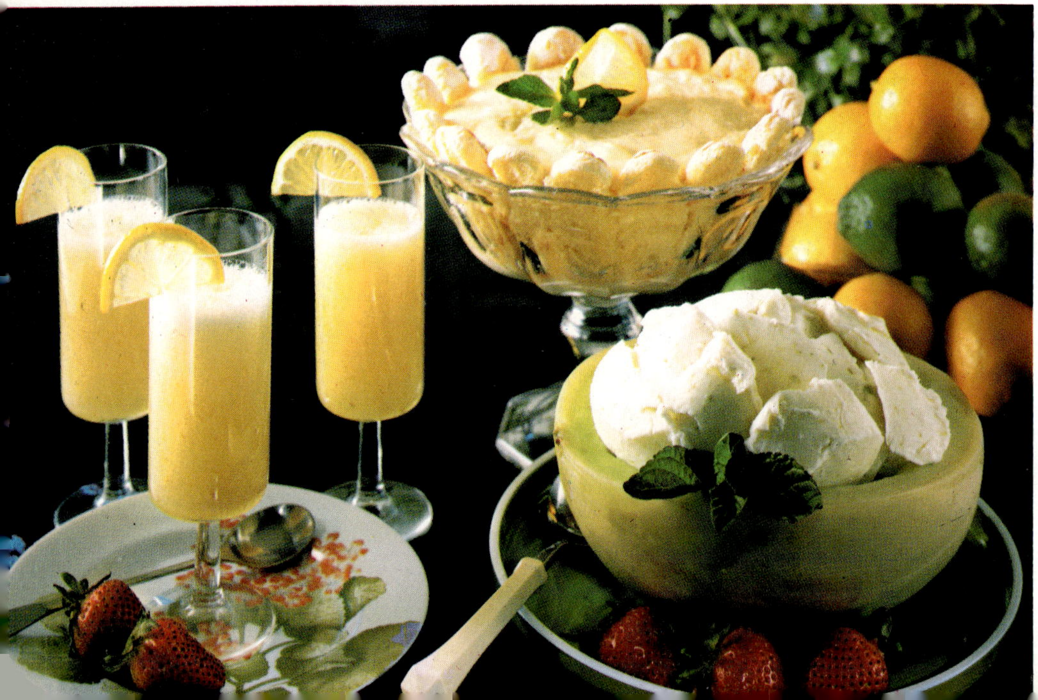

WOMAN'S DAY STUDIO

IRWIN HOROWITZ

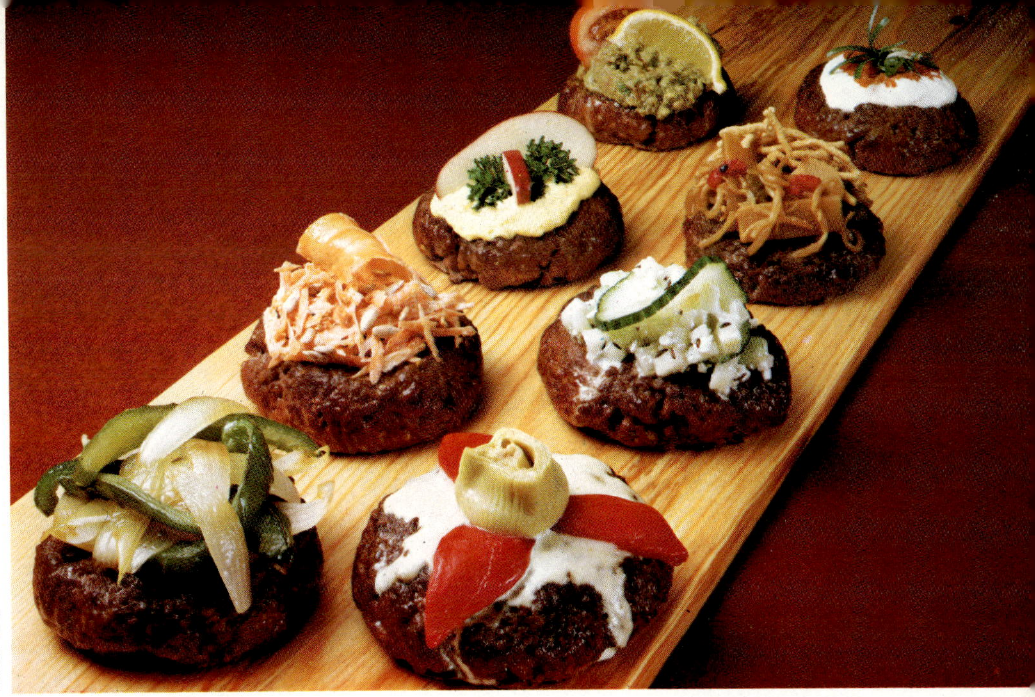

Topped with a zesty, colorful garnish, hamburgers can be nutritious, delicious, and eye-catching!

Use color and imagination to enhance your morning meals. Insert orange slices between portions of small pancakes served on a bright blue plate; nestle blueberry muffins in a basket lined with a checkered cloth; add chunks of honeydew melon to perk up a bowl of blueberries.

WILL ROUSSEAU

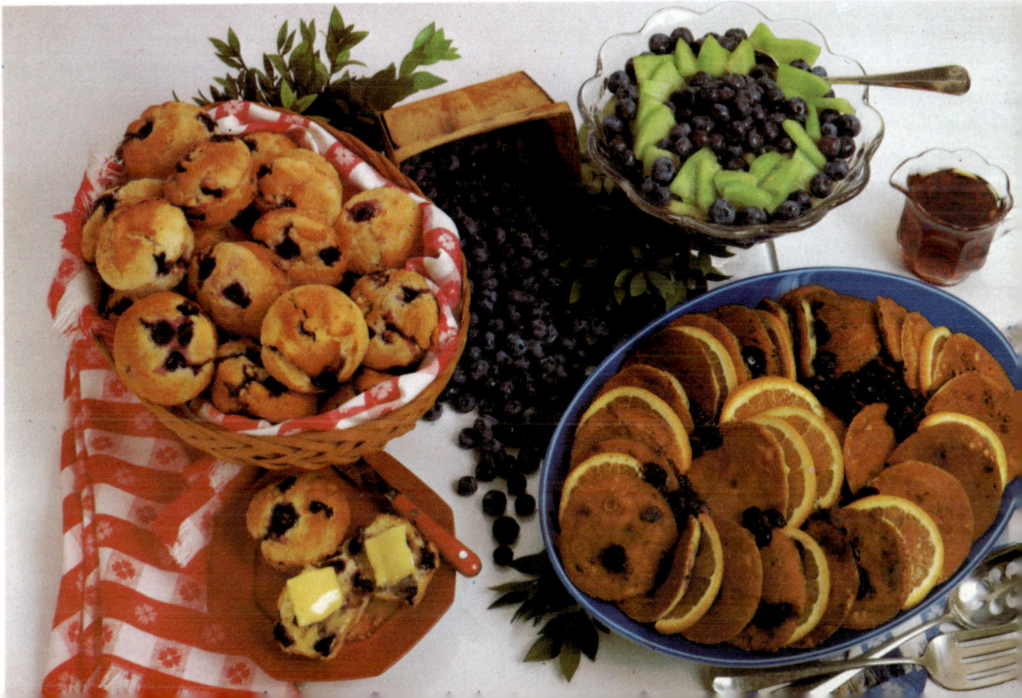

An attractive setting and food that looks appealing can turn a dieter's dilemma into a delightful experience.

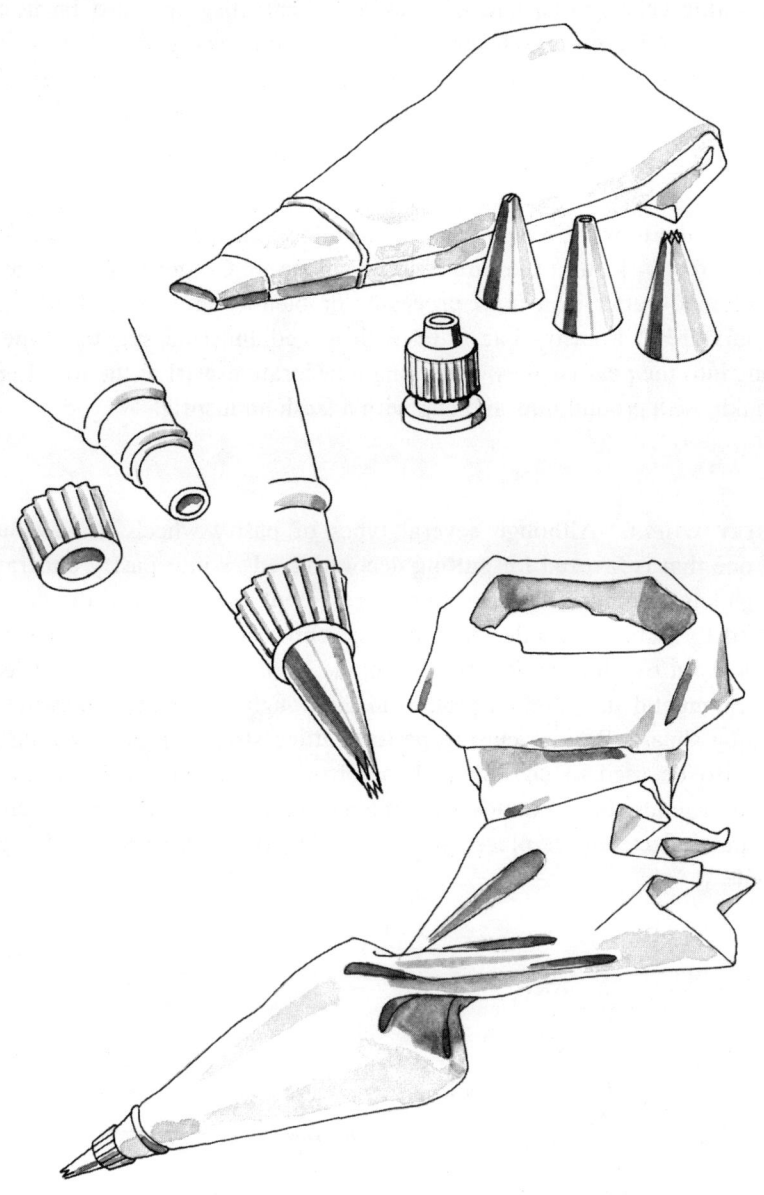

Pastry Bags

decorating cakes, tarts, and pastries, the pastry bag can also be used to shape and fill cream puffs and éclairs, to stuff celery and hard-cooked eggs, to pipe decorative flowers, stars, and patterns onto canapés and hors d'oeuvre, or to pipe mashed potatoes into decorative borders.

• Slice the tops off 6 ripe pears and hollow out the cores with an apple corer. Process 1 cup of crumbled blue cheese or Gorgonzola with ½ cup of softened butter in a food processor or blender until smooth. Transfer the mixture to a pastry bag fitted with a medium-sized star tip. Pipe the filling into the pear cavities, squeezing a decorative swirl at the top. Lightly sprinkle with ground nuts and cap with a fresh mint sprig.

PASTRY WHEEL Although several types of pastry wheels are available, the one that is favored for cutting decorative edges into pastry and ravioli dough has a crimped metal cutting wheel about 1½ inches in diameter attached to a sturdy wooden handle. The entire length of the gadget measures about 6½ inches. Because the blade of this wheel is jagged, it leaves an ornamental saw-toothed pattern in the dough as it cuts, somewhat like pinking shears. Besides cutting perfect lattice strips for pies and tarts, it can also be used to cut other shapes from the dough, such as squares, hearts, rounds, or diamonds with pinked edges. These decorative shapes can then effectively be placed on top of pies, tarts, pastries, and foods en croûte.

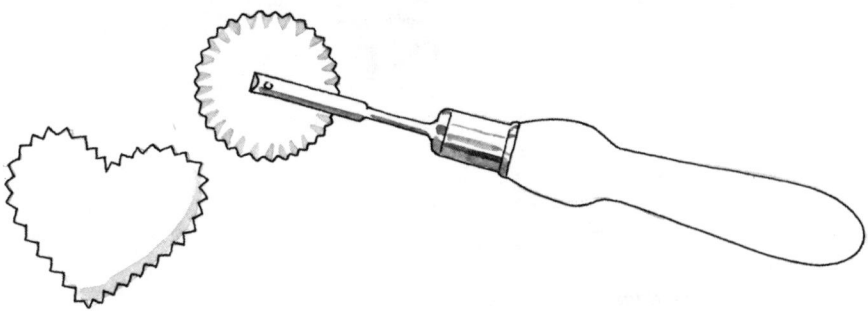

PIE BIRD   This ceramic blackbird with chirping yellow beak comes from England and is as much of a delight to the eye as it is in its function. When its head peeps through the top crust of a pie, it acts as a steam-release chimney, preventing the pie juices from overflowing. To use, line the pie plate with the bottom crust and set the 4-inch-tall bird in the center. Arrange the filling around the bird and cover with the top crust, poking a small hole in the center so that the bird's head comes through the pastry. Bake pie as your recipe directs.

PIE SPATULA   This wedge-shaped tin device is positioned in the pie plate before the dough. It serves as a marker and a guide for the first perfect cut and as a lift-out server for the first perfect piece.

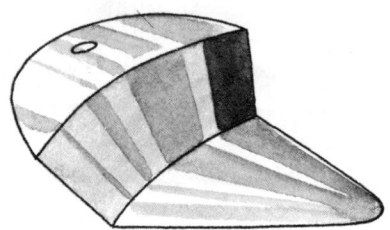

PIE WEIGHTS These aluminum pellets are useful when baking a pie shell without a filling because they prevent the dough from "bubbling" or cracking in the hot oven. To use, line a pie plate or flan ring with pastry and lightly prick it all over with a fork. Cut a piece of parchment paper or foil the same size as the pastry and arrange it in the pie dish on top of the dough. Sprinkle the pie weights evenly over the surface of the paper, then bake until the crust is golden. Remove shell from oven and lift out the paper with the pie weights, being careful not to touch them until they have cooled. One or two pounds of uncooked rice or dried beans may be used instead of aluminum pie weights to accomplish the same purpose, but the paper holding the rice or beans must be lifted out halfway through baking so that the crust can brown.

PINEAPPLE CUTTER Cut the top and bottom off a fresh pineapple, then stand it on a cutting board. The stainless steel cutter removes the skin and core from the fruit in one downward, thrusting motion, leaving a sweet and juicy cylinder that can then be sliced into rings or wedges. The cutter is approximately 7 inches tall.

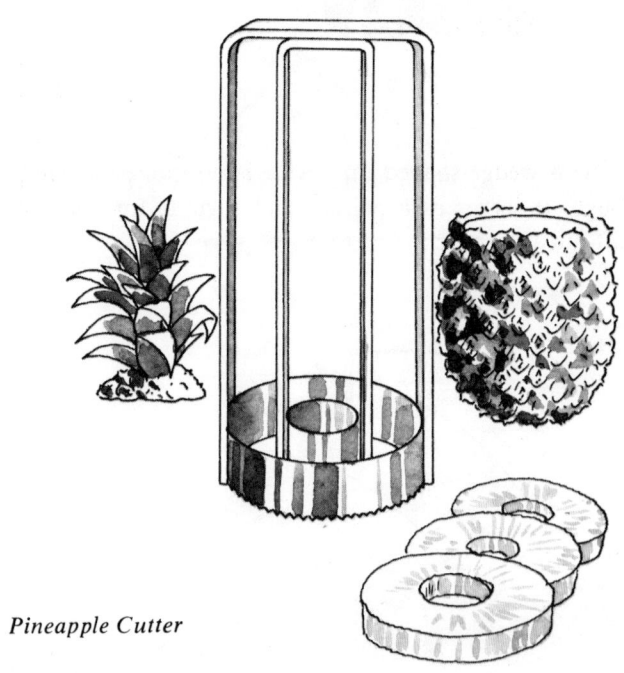

Pineapple Cutter

- Place a golden pineapple ring in the center of a large blue plate. Place a scoop of cottage cheese on top of the pineapple. Top the mound of cheese with a perfect red strawberry and stud the entire mound with seedless green grapes.

- Place several pineapple rings in a lightly buttered baking dish. Top each with a scoop of mashed sweet potatoes. Stud the top of the potato mounds with miniature marshmallows. Place in a moderately hot oven, about 350° F., for about 10 minutes, until the marshmallows are melted. Lift rings out of dish with a spatula and use to garnish a baked ham or roast turkey.

RADISH ROSETTE PRESS   This is actually a dual-purpose tool—it punches out perfect radish roses with just one swift press, and it also has a sharp v-shaped blade that can be used to cut scalloped edges around citrus shells. Crafted of cast aluminum, the tong-shaped device is approximately 6 inches long and consists of two handles joined by a pivot. At the open end of the bottom handle there is a slightly indented cup to hold the radish. At the open end of the top handle is a sturdy circular frame for the sharp stainless steel cutting blades. The secondary v-shaped blade is positioned at the very tip of the tool.

To make a radish rosette, trim the stem and root end from a large radish. Place it vertically in the cup of the tool underneath the cutting framework and squeeze the handles together. The gadget cuts right into the heart of the radish, creating instant "petals." Soaking the radish roses in ice water for a few hours will cause the petals to spread out in full bloom. Rosettes may also be carved from 1¼-inch lengths of raw carrots, parsnips, baby zucchini, or yellow squash.

- Pile radish roses into a wicker basket and nestle a cup of your favorite dip in the center of the pile.

To make scalloped citrus shells, cut an orange in half and scoop out the pulp. Press the v-shaped blade of the cutter all around the rim of the hollowed fruit. Refill the decorated shell with marmalade or jam for breakfast or with small berries for dessert.

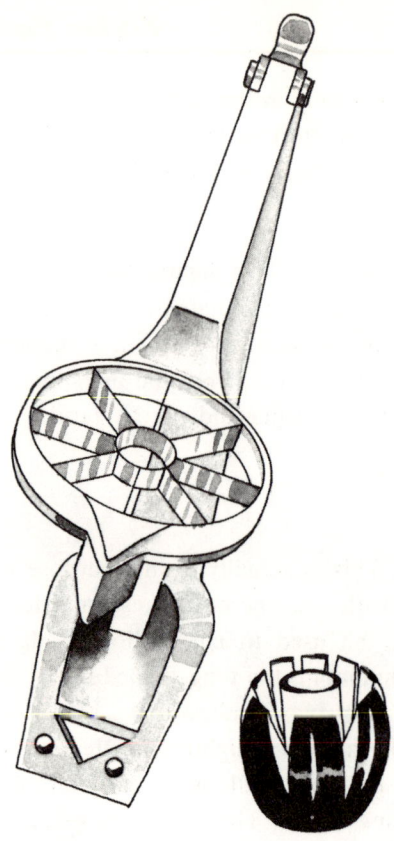

Radish Rosette Press

• Pile whole strawberries into hollowed grapefruit shells, bright red Bing cherries into hollowed orange shells, seedless green grapes into orange shells, and blueberries into lemon shells. Arrange on a large platter with two or three varieties of cheese.

RADISH SPIRAL CUTTER This gadget cuts radishes and other firm vegetables into fascinating spiral coils that make irresistible additions to any number of cold platters and salads. The tool has a circular plastic loop handle that is attached to a very sharp stainless steel blade, about 4½ inches in overall length. A pointed spiral screw, about 1½ inches long, protrudes at a right angle from the tip of the blade. Some radish cutter models, but not all, have a 5-inch metal spindle (resembling a skewer) that fits into the top of the spiral screw to keep the radish coil in place as you cut. To use, trim the ends from a large radish and insert the spiral screw into one end. If provided, insert the spindle in place, on top of the screw. Holding the radish firmly, rotate the blade around and around, carving a coil as you work. Raw carrots, parsnips, firm zucchini, and yellow squash are just some of the other vegetables suited to this tool.

• Carve several radish spirals. Position them around a platter of cold cuts and tuck 2 or 3 raw baby spinach leaves underneath each radish spiral.

• Enliven a plain green salad with spirals cut from 1½-inch lengths of raw carrot.

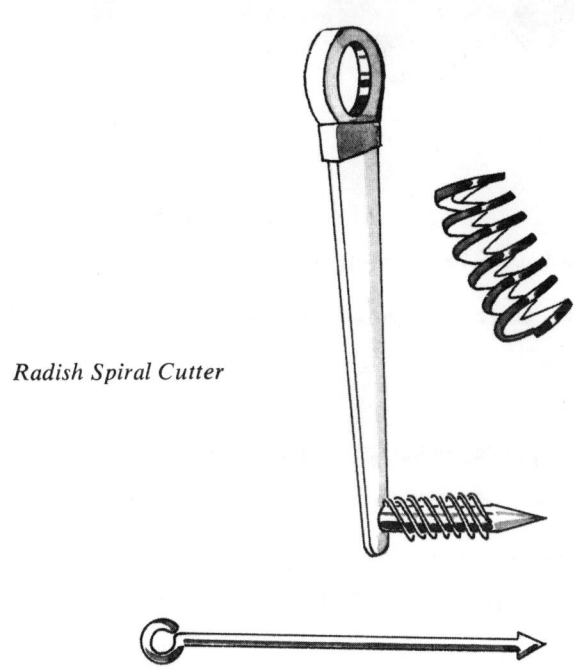

Radish Spiral Cutter

ROLLING MINCER This device makes short work of chopping fresh green herbs, sliced onions, garlic, and shallots. Five sharp stainless steel circular blades attached to a single axle are covered with a plastic or metal shield. The tool is rolled back and forth over the food to be chopped on a cutting board until the desired texture is obtained. A sprinkling of minced greenery is one of the easiest ways to enhance the eye appeal, aroma, and flavor of foods.

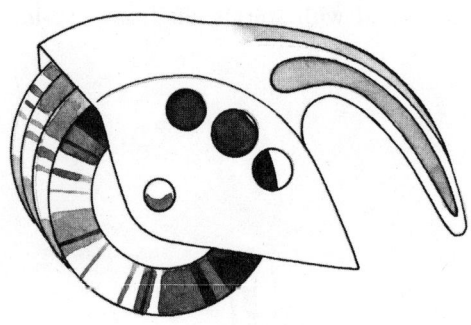

Try:

• Minced fresh basil over hot buttered noodles.

• Fresh chopped chives over potato or cucumber salad.

• Sprinkles of fresh dill over tomato wedges, feta cheese chunks, and black olives tossed with virgin olive oil.

• Verdant green parsley flakes crowning steamed rosy-red new potatoes.

• A smattering of tarragon on broiled swordfish steaks.

• Mosaic flecks of green and red bell peppers over macaroni salad.

• A mixture of minced basil and chives floating on a sea of chilled tomato soup.

• Finely minced celery leaves adrift in a clear consommé.

• Feathery fennel bulb leaves strewn over hot spaghetti sauce.

Kitchen Equipment   43

SHRIMP CLEANERS   Many people dislike preparing fresh shrimp at home because of the lengthy shelling and deveining process involved. However, with one of the several models of shrimp cleaners available from gourmet specialty shops, this task no longer need be dreaded. Gadgets have been designed that shell and devein the crustaceans, raw or cooked, in one easy motion. The pointed tip of the implement is inserted between the flesh and the shell at the head end, then worked along the back curve of the shrimp toward the tail end. This both splits the shell and removes the dark vein at the same time. Peel the broken shell off with your fingers, but leave the tail attached for visual effect.

• Arrange a whole, clean celery stalk with leaves intact in the center of a large green plate. Hook the curved part of 4 or 5 cold, fat pink (cooked and peeled) shrimp over the celery stalk at 1-inch intervals. Fill a hollowed lemon half with mayonnaise and set it on the plate. Serve cold.

• Slice off the top third of a straight-standing, medium-sized green bell pepper. Reserve the top and hollow out the pepper. Place it in the center of a medium-sized plate and fill it with cocktail sauce or lemon mayonnaise. Hook 4 or 5 medium-sized cold shrimp (cooked and peeled) around the edge of the pepper. Lay the pepper top cut side up next to the pepper and shrimp arrangement. Set a juicy yellow lemon wedge next to the pepper top. Serve cold.

STRAWBERRY HULLER   Nothing else in your kitchen can possibly compare with this tiny metal pincer for neatly and quickly removing the stems and leaves from strawberries without cutting into the flesh of the fruit. The 2½-inch-long huller is comprised of a single flat strip of stainless steel, bent in half like a tweezer. It is uniquely functional, easy to use, and quite inexpensive.

• Serve a bright green spinach and bacon salad adorned with whole red strawberries in a large glass bowl.

• Place a square serving of gingerbread on a bright red plate. Top the cake with a dollop of pink applesauce and one large red strawberry.

TOMATO CUTTER This white plastic drum houses 5 v-shaped stainless steel teeth that appear when the handle at its base is turned. With a twist of the wrist this gadget cuts small tomatoes, turnips, beets, large radishes, and peeled hard-cooked eggs into two perfect star-shaped pieces. It will work equally well on any firm-fleshed fruit or vegetable that is up to 2¼ inches in diameter. Use the intriguing vandyke (very much like that beard) shapes anywhere an appropriate festive garnish is needed, such as on salads and around platters.

• Cut 4 whole Harvard beets with the tomato cutter. Arrange them cut side up on a bed of lightly dressed watercress. Sprinkle the beets with a few shreds of grated orange rind.

• Island a star-cut hard-cooked egg in a minute pool of pink Russian dressing. Sprinkle with alfalfa sprouts.

Tomato Cutter

VEGETABLE PEELERS You can remove the skin from any vegetable or fruit with a sharp paring knife, but specialized peelers have been developed to help you accomplish this task with greater ease and speed. The most popular have a movable swivel-action blade that automatically adjusts itself to the natural contours of the vegetable as you work. French versions of this tool have a wide handle positioned perpendicular to the swivel-action blade, which is lightly pulled across the surface of the vegetable. The elongated handle of the standard American model is an extension of the swivel-action blade, and the shape of the tool is better suited to a shucking motion. In addition, the tip of the standard American model is shaped like a spade so that it can be used to dig out potato eyes and any other bad spots sometimes found on vegetables. None of these peelers can be resharpened once the blade becomes dull, but they are relatively inexpensive and should be replaced once they fail to cut a thin, neat peel.

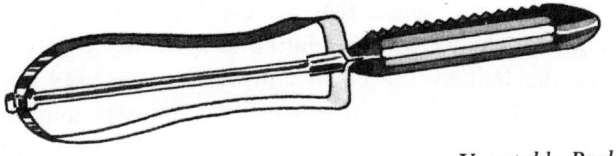

Vegetable Peeler

• Select a large lemon and, starting at one end, begin to peel it in a long strip, about ½ inch wide. The standard American peeler is best for this job. Try to peel the entire lemon in one continuous strip. Make a lemon rose by wrapping the peel around and around into a coil. Secure the coil with a toothpick, if necessary. Use the lemon rose to adorn a poached fish fillet sauced with beurre blanc. Tuck a few watercress leaves under the rose to enhance the effect.

• The next time you serve turnips, make turnip roses from the peeled skin that can be used to adorn your serving platter. Cut off the top and tail from each turnip. Use a standard American peeler and, beginning at one end of a turnip, carve off a continuous strip of peel, about ½ inch wide. Carefully curl the strip of peel to resemble a rose. Secure the coiled rose with a toothpick and soak the blossom in ice water until ready to serve. Drain on paper toweling and tuck a few sprigs of flat-leafed parsley under the roses for added color. The lavender blush of the turnips makes an unusually effective decoration.

• Sprinkle carrot and parsnip curls over a green salad for added color and texture. Using a standard American peeler, cut lengthwise paper-thin slices from scrubbed carrots and parsnips. Roll up the strips and fasten with toothpicks. Chill in a bowl of ice water until serving time. Remove picks. If desired, place a green olive in the center of each parsnip curl and a ripe olive in the center of each carrot curl.

WONDERBALL   This 2½-inch-diameter fine mesh ball is made of stainless steel so that it will not absorb food odors or impart a metallic taste. The sphere is suspended from a 7-inch chain with a hook on the opposite end so that it can be hung from the rim of a pot without getting lost in the depths of whatever you're cooking. Open the hinged ball and fill it with the ingredients for a bouquet garni or other herbs and spices called for when seasoning a stew, sauce, or soup. Because the seasonings are contained within the fine wire mesh, they are easy to remove before serving, and there will be no chance of biting into a stray clove or brittle bay leaf. Simply remove the ball by the chain and discard the used condiments. The ball can also be used as an excellent tea infuser, imprisoning the loose leaves so that the tea will not have to be strained before pouring.

• Place a small strip of orange peel inside the wonderball and suspend it in a pot of simmering beef stew where it will impart a delicate, exotic flavor.

• Put a few mint leaves into the wonderball and suspend into a pan of simmering garden peas.

• Make fresh-brewed coffee for one! Place a measure of ground coffee into the ball and suspend in a cup of hot boiled water until it turns the desired strength.

✸

ZUCCHINI CORER   This specialized cutting tool has a 6-inch-long trough-shaped blade attached to either a wooden or a plastic handle. It can be used to hollow out any straight, elongated vegetable such as zucchini, summer squash, cucumbers, potatoes, or small eggplants, and it works equally well on apples or pears. Insert the corer into one end of the vegetable or fruit and rotate the implement slightly as you force it through to the other end.

• Select several medium-sized baking potatoes and carve a lengthwise tunnel through each with the corer. Insert a precooked sausage link into each cavity and bake potatoes in a moderate oven, 350° F., until tender. Cut the baked potato surprises into ¾-inch slices and arrange them on a plate in an overlapping semicircular pattern.

• Hollow out zucchini and stuff with a Roquefort and cream cheese mixture. Chill thoroughly and slice into ½-inch rounds to be served as a refreshing snack or salad garnish.

• Score cucumber skins with a fork and then hollow out the center with the corer. Stuff the cavity with pimiento- and chive-flecked cream cheese. Slice ½ inch thick on the bias to obtain delightful oval hors d'oeuvre.

Zucchini Corer

Coeur à la Crème

Culinary Molds

Molded foods, hot or cold, always seem to fascinate people and create a fabulous effect at the table. They have the ability to turn the simplest ingredients into fanciful shapes that captivate everyone's attention. Surprisingly, there are many containers in your home which can be used to make very attractive molded presentations. Cups, glasses, jars, bowls, cans, and pans are just a few such items. Make sure that the rim and sides of the selected container are not smaller in circumference than the bottom. Otherwise, it will be impossible to unmold.

• Bake homemade bread in an unglazed clay flowerpot for an unusual but delightful shape.

• The deliciously creamy dessert called coeur à la crème is traditionally molded in a perforated ceramic heart. If you care to improvise, substitute a woven basket or bowl-shaped strainer for the heart. (The container you select must have some holes at the bottom to allow liquid to drain through.) Line the basket or sieve with a double layer of dampened cheesecloth before filling with the cheese mixture. Place over a bowl to catch the dripping whey, cover with plastic wrap, and refrigerate overnight before unmolding. Surround the mound with crushed strawberries or raspberries.

• Mold a coeur à la crème mixture in a low-sided oval basket lined with a double layer of wet cheesecloth. Place in a baking dish to catch the drips, cover with plastic wrap, and refrigerate overnight. Unmold onto a lime-green platter strewn with grape leaves. Stud the entire molded dessert with halved and seeded purple grapes, so that it resembles a bunch of grapes.

STORE-BOUGHT MOLDS   Some foods come molded and packaged in containers directly from the store. With a little imagination, many of these natural shapes can be put to decorative use.

• Unmold a pint of vanilla ice cream (without disturbing its shape) onto the center of a chilled cake plate. Press lady fingers upright around the sides of the ice cream and halved lady fingers over the top. Generously brush the surface of the lady fingers with slightly warmed apricot preserves. Arrange drained apricot halves around the base of the bombe and pipe rosettes of whipped cream between the mounds of fruit. Voilà! A molded confection without fuss.

• Open a can of jellied cranberry sauce at both ends and gently push out the whole shape. Set the cranberry cylinder on a crystal plate and cut the jellied sauce into ½-inch slices. Push the slices so that they lie in an overlapping pattern. Slice two navel oranges into ¼-inch rounds and insert the orange slices between the cranberry slices. Surround the sandwiched red and orange creation with alternating walnut halves and seedless green grapes.

• Unmold a canned ham and cut it into ¾-inch slices almost, but not quite, all the way through. Cut several pineapple rings in half and insert a halved slice into each of the slits in the ham. Place in an oven-to-table baking dish. Arrange remaining pineapple around the base of the ham. Glaze and bake as directed, until heated through.

INDIVIDUAL MOLDS   Individually molded portions of food, savory or sweet, always seem to lend a personal touch to a meal, as though they were created with each person in mind. There are a number of specialized molds that fall into this category. Their obvious charm is underscored by the fact that, regardless of their intended purpose, they are all extremely versatile. Many can be used interchangeably for baking meats, custards, little cakes, or puddings and for molding all sorts of cold dishes including aspics, mousses, soufflés, and ice cream.

BABA *or* TIMBALE MOLD   The classic baba is a little rum-soaked cake made from a rich yeast dough studded with raisins. Timbales are usually savory baked custards or mousses, individually molded in the traditional timbale mound. The shape of the mold resembles a large thimble with slightly sloping sides, varying in capacity from ⅓ to ½ cup. It is available in stainless steel or in a less expensive tinned steel. The metal makes the mold suitable for both cooked or chilled dishes.

• Bake pale pumpkin custard timbales, unmold, and top with glossy walnut halves. Arrange on a bed of lightly steamed spinach.

• Jell individual strawberry bavarians in timbale molds. Turn out on a lilac-colored plate and surround with snowy-white shredded coconut. Top each mound with a halved strawberry, cut side down.

BRIOCHE MOLDS   Brioches are tender, fluted rolls baked from a rich yeast dough. Classically shaped with sloping scalloped sides, the distinctive tinned steel molds for baking brioches are available in individual, 3-cup, or 6-cup capacities. The molds can also be used to form mousses, crème caramel, and other molded foods, savory or sweet.

Brioche Mold

• Prepare individual portions of pink salmon mousse in brioche molds. When chilled and set, turn out onto a lime-green plate. Place a large green caper in each fluted hollow and top the mousse with a smidgen of red lumpfish caviar.

• Prepare individual portions of tomato aspic in brioche molds. Arrange a young Bibb lettuce leaf on each chocolate-brown salad plate. Unmold the shimmering red aspic onto the leaf. Cut pitted black olives into rings and arrange on top of each aspic.

EGG EN GELÉE RAMEKINS   Shallow, oval molds of 5-ounce capacity may be made of tinned steel, stainless steel, porcelain, or glass. They are used for molding cooked eggs in transparent aspic. Cover the bottom of each mold with ⅛ to ¼ inch of aspic. Decorate with feathery sprigs of dill, fennel, or tarragon or with tiny shapes cut from colorful vegetables with aspic cutters. When the aspic is almost firm and the design has set, place a shelled semi-hard-cooked egg (firm white, soft yolk) in the mold. Carefully spoon in more aspic until the ramekin is full. Chill until set and unmold. The molds may also be used for shaping oval mounds of cooked rice, or for baking individual custards, bread puddings, or appetizer servings of pot pies.

• Prepare individual terrines of chicken liver pâté in the ramekins. Arrange 3 thin slices of radish and a small sprig of dill in a decorative pattern on top of the pâté. Spoon aspic over and chill until set. No need to unmold. Place a ramekin on a pretty serving plate and surround with toast triangles.

• Prepare a mixture of sautéed scallops and mushrooms in a light cheese and cream sauce. Ladle the mixture into the ramekins and top with rolled-out dough for flaky pastry. Use aspic cutters to cut out designs from leftover strips of dough and arrange them over the top crust before baking. Cut a small hole in the center for the steam to escape. Bake in a 400° F. preheated oven until crust is golden brown, about 12 to 15 minutes. Place hot ramekins in the center of your serving plates.

❋

ICE SCULPTURE MOLDS   A statue of sculpted ice can turn a table spread with the simplest foods into a special attraction. If you're skilled enough to make ice cubes, you can easily construct a frozen masterpiece with a kit containing a disposable plastic mold. The finished ice forms average 9 to 10 inches high, but your freezer must be large enough to hold the box that the mold comes in—full instructions are included. The "cast" of characters available include a dolphin, a seal, a frog, a polar bear, a Christmas tree, a penguin, or a family grouping of penguins. The frozen pièces de résistance are not only beautiful to look at but functional as well, serving to keep your chilled foods and beverages cold.

• Fill a large platter with crushed ice and set a seaworthy ice statue, such as a dolphin or seal, in the center. Arrange sprigs of fresh dill, resembling seaweed, over the ice bed, and place large lemon wedges around the base of the statue. This makes an ideal stage for cold clams or oysters on the half shell, fish or lobster salad served in scallop shells, or whole cooked, cold shrimp or crab legs.

• Stand a frozen frog or family of penguins in the center of a punch bowl for a children's party.

• Island an ice sculpture in the center of a large crystal bowl filled with jellied consommé or cold soup for a summer party.

• Surround an ice sculpture with small mounds of whole strawberries, clusters of seedless grapes, melon and cheese cubes.

✻

SAVARIN *or* RING-SHAPED MOLDS A savarin is a ring-shaped dessert cake made from yeast dough. Once baked, turned out, and cooled, it is usually basted with kirsch syrup and glazed with apricot preserves. The center ring may then be filled with whipped cream or custard and the cake surrounded with fresh or poached fruits. Savarin molds are available in several sizes, including small ones for individual servings. The classic ring shape makes the mold suitable for other attractive dishes such as molded gelatin salads and desserts or baked vegetable custards or puddings.

• Bake individual servings of meat loaf in savarin molds. Turn out onto orange dinner plates, centering each mold. Fill the ring cavity with steamed green peas and pipe a decorative border of mashed potatoes around the base of each meat ring.

• Ladle ⅛ inch of transparent aspic into the bottom of each savarin mold. Arrange a pattern of sliced, cooked carrots over the aspic and chill until set. Add an additional ¼-inch layer of aspic and carrots and chill. When set, add a layer of aspic and steamed green peas; chill until set. Finish with a layer of aspic and cooked yellow corn kernels. Chill until set. Unmold the salads on a bed of shredded lettuce and fill each ring cavity with homemade mayonnaise sprinkled with chopped parsley or dill.

Savarin or Ring-Shaped Molds

BUTTER MOLDS Charm everyone with butter molded in the shape of a rabbit, a chicken, a scalloped seashell, or a cavorting fish. It's easy to create individual butter sculptures about 1½ inches tall with two-part, bisque-fired ceramic molds. They are sold in sets of four in gourmet specialty departments or stores. Just pack the small pottery molds with slightly softened butter, refrigerate until firm, and unmold. Store in the refrigerator until serving time. Allow one or two butter shapes per person.

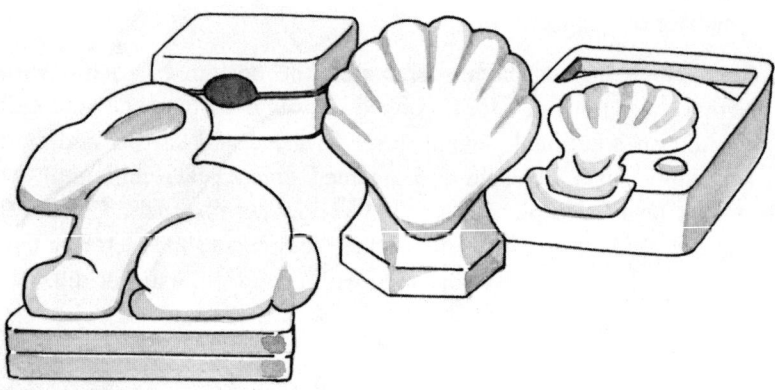

• Mold several scalloped seashells, allowing one for each serving. Place a generous sprig of fresh dill in the center of each bread plate. Arrange a butter seashell on one side of the greenery, with a dinner roll on the opposite side.

• Mold several rabbit forms, allowing one for each serving. Place a roll and a rabbit on each bread plate and surround the butter sculpture with matchstick nibbles of raw carrot.

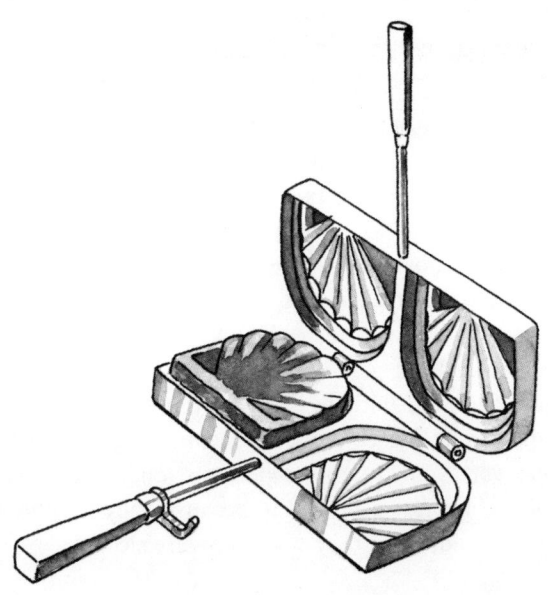

CROQUE MONSIEUR TOASTING IRON A croque monsieur by any other name is a grilled sandwich raised to the highest level of foreign culinary intrigue. Thinly sliced cheese, such as American, Swiss, or muenster, or grated Gruyère or cheddar can be toasted between buttered bread slices in combination with ham, chicken, turkey, bacon, corned beef, vegetables, or fruit. The toasting iron imprints a scalloped shell design onto the toasted sandwich, which makes it look as appealing as it tastes. The iron is available in single or double sandwich molds made of cast aluminum with heatproof handles. Overall length measures approximately 12 inches. To use, assemble the sandwich, buttering the bread on the outside. Place it within the mold and set it on the heated stove, either gas or electric, until toasted a golden brown. Serve hot.

Instructions are included, but you might try these tasty combinations:

• Buttered whole wheat bread sprinkled with crumbled blue cheese and filled with a layer of drained sliced peaches. Garnish the plate with two whole strawberries.

• Buttered rye bread layered with creamy mozzarella, fresh chopped basil and anchovies, and sliced garden tomatoes. Garnish with 3 black olives set in a nest of alfalfa sprouts.

• Buttered rye bread filled with sliced pastrami, tomatoes, and Gruyère strewn with sauerkraut. Garnish the plate with a hollowed lime shell filled with Russian or Thousand Island dressing.

GELATIN OR ICE CREAM MOLDS These are available in many materials (glass, ceramic, metal, etc.) and in hundreds of shapes and sizes, from the smallest timbale to grand and fanciful turrets. While the design of a mold should be appropriate to the food it contains, such as a seafood mousse in a fish form, most molds are versatile and can be used interchangeably for aspics, mousses, or ice cream. The simpler the shape of the mold, the easier it will be to turn out. Deep, peaked, or pointed cone molds should be avoided for gelatins made with a lot of cream, because they are difficult to unmold without spoiling the shape. Metal molds are preferred by many cooks for cold foods because the material is easy to handle and reacts very quickly to temperature changes. Glass, ceramic, and porcelain molds are not as popular because they are breakable and can be difficult to unmold, since they warm up very slowly.

• Line a large melon-shaped mold with pistachio ice cream and freeze until firm. Pack raspberry sherbet into the center of the pistachio-lined mold and freeze until firm. Unmold onto an oval platter and garnish with sugar-frosted cranberries and mint sprigs.

• Prepare a lemon snow in a star-shaped mold and chill until set. Unmold onto a bright yellow plate. Arrange fresh violet blossoms on top of the lemon snow and place small clusters of violets in between the star points at the base of the mold.

PÂTÉ MOLDS Meat loaf anyone? Pâté is simply the French word for one of the most popular dishes in America! Any ground or chopped meat can be used singly or in combination, as well as liver, poultry, game, or fish. And any meat loaf can be elevated to new heights by layering the meat mixture with hard-cooked eggs, whole chicken livers, sausages, or slices of ham or tongue before baking. Americans are used to cooking their meat loaves in a mounded free form or in a loaf pan, but special pâté molds are available to give your meat loaf a totally new and elegant look.

A pâté or meat loaf that is cooked and served cold directly from its baking dish is called a terrine. Just about any baking dish of appropriate size is suitable for this purpose—an oval casserole, a soufflé dish, an ovenproof mixing bowl, a bean pot, or a loaf pan. Or you may wish to buy a special terrine mold to be used solely for that purpose. To use, completely line the mold with thinly sliced bacon or fat, allowing the slices to overlap the edge of the dish. Half fill the terrine with meat mixture. If desired, add a layer of sliced ham, chicken, or turkey. Pack remaining filling into mold and completely cover the top with the overlapping slices of bacon, adding more if necessary. Arrange a few whole bay leaves on top of the bacon slices for added flavor and eye appeal. Cover the terrine with a lid or aluminum foil and bake according to your recipe in a large pan partially filled with boiling water. Once cooked, remove the terrine and allow it to cool, weighted down, if so specified in your recipe. Refrigerate until thoroughly chilled. Slice to serve and garnish each portion with crunchy gherkins and tiny pickled onions.

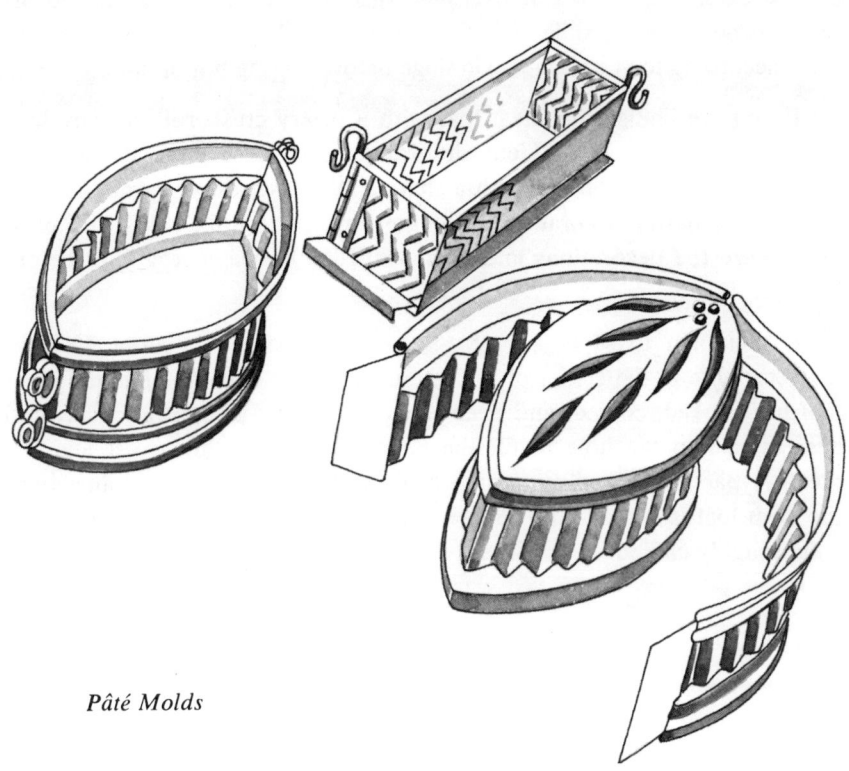

Pâté Molds

A hinged pâté mold is the thing to use if you wish to serve your meat loaf encased in a golden crust or sheathed in rosy strips of bacon. As the cooked pâté cools, it shrinks away from the sides of the pan, making the unmolding as easy as pie. The hinged pâté mold works on a principle similar to that of a spring-form pan. It has collapsible sides that solve the problem of removing the pâté from the pan after baking without having to invert it. The mold is made of separate pieces of tinned steel—one for the bottom and one for each side. The pieces fit snugly together and are held in place by metal clamps. The special molds are available in either a rectangular or ridged oval shape, and in a small assortment of sizes. To use, assemble the hinged mold and completely line with rolled-out pastry dough or thinly sliced bacon, making sure that there is a generous overhang. Pack with meat mixture, layering with sausage links or hard-cooked eggs, if desired. Lift overhanging pastry dough or bacon and arrange as neatly as possible over the top of the filling. Trim or flute edges. Bake according to your recipe. Unhinge before serving hot or cold.

• If you are lining your meat loaf with a pastry crust, roll out any leftover scraps of dough and cut decorative shapes, such as flowers and leaves, with aspic cutters or with a sharp knife. Use raw egg white as glue to stick the pastry decorations onto the top crust of the uncooked meat loaf. Glaze the decorations and crust with lightly beaten egg yolk before baking.

• If you plan to serve a pastry-lined meat loaf cold, cut a ¾-inch-diameter hole in the center of the top crust before baking. After the meat loaf has cooked, cooled, and been unmolded, pour a slightly set flavored beef aspic into the hole to fill the air space between the crust and the meat. A parsley-flecked or tomato aspic will add even more drama once the meat loaf is sliced. Refrigerate until the aspic is firm and the meat loaf is thoroughly chilled.

❋

Knives

Good-quality, balanced knives are essential to any well-equipped kitchen. Most of all, knives should be sharpened each time they are used; knife sharpening should become a habit. Generally speaking, a "basic wardrobe" or a practical selection of useful knives consists of five different blades:

> Paring knife—3- and 4-inch blade
> Chef's knife—8-, 10-, or 12-inch blade
> Slicing knife—10- or 12-inch blade
> Serrated knife—8-inch blade
> Boning knife—6-inch blade

This basic knife selection is really all you need to perform most cutting tasks. However, there are other knives available for specialized or delicate cutting work which you may also find useful.

PARING KNIFE Most cooks find this to be the most useful knife in the kitchen. It can be used to cube, diagonal-cut, dice, french-cut, julienne, mince, pare, peel, score, etc. It is generally used for cutting small items of food that need peeling, shaping, or decorative carving. The short, sharp blade with a pointy tip can even double as a mini-chopper.

• To french-cut green beans is to give them a unique texture that cannot be accomplished by any other cutting technique. Trim the ends off the beans and remove any strings. Halve each bean lengthwise between the seams. Cook beans, covered, in a steamer set 1 inch above boiling water, just until tender—about 5 to 10 minutes, depending on the tenderness of the beans. Toss cooked beans with butter to serve hot or with vinaigrette and allow to cool to serve cold.

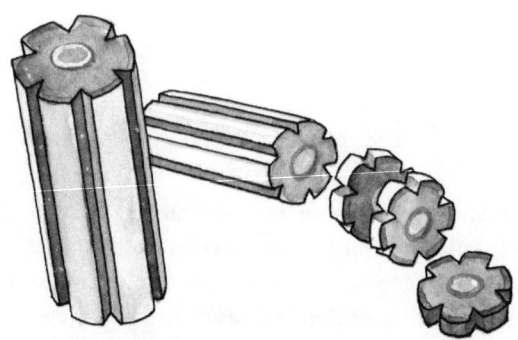

• To make appealing carrot flowers, peel whole carrots and cut them in half. Parboil the 3- to 4-inch long carrot cylinders for about 10 minutes, or until they are slightly tender. Refresh under cold running water until they are cool enough to handle. Using a sharp paring knife, cut 6 evenly spaced wedges, each about ⅛-inch deep, along the length of each carrot cylinder. Slice the notched cylinders into ⅛-inch coins to make flower shapes. Sprinkle the flowers over a salad. Or, to serve hot, sauté them in melted butter. Arrange the hot carrot flowers around the rim of each dinner plate and sprinkle them with finely minced parsley.

• Turn Jerusalem artichokes (sunchokes) into sculptured ovals. Peel and then cut the sunchokes into chunks ¾ × ¾ × 1 inch. Use your paring knife to carve the pieces into evenly sized oval shapes. Steam ovaled sunchokes just until tender, about 5 minutes. Toss with butter and sprinkle with chopped walnuts for added flavor and texture. Arrange 4 dressed sunchoke ovals in an arc around the outside curve of a broiled double lamb chop.

CHEF'S KNIFE   This knife is designed to be the best chopper and mincer in your kitchen. Grasp the knife by the handle with one hand, and steady the blade by lightly resting the fingers of your other hand *over* the tip. Holding the pointed end down, pump the handle up and down over the vegetables to be chopped or minced on a cutting board. The back blade should be deep enough so that you do not rap your knuckles when using this rocking motion.

SLICING *or* CARVING KNIFE   The long straight blade of a slicing knife is just the right size and shape for carving large cuts of cooked meat, such as roast leg of lamb or a thick broiled steak. It is also the best blade to use for thin slices of flank steak or corned beef cut on the bias. As with other knives, sharpness is essential for a neat, clean cut.

SERRATED KNIFE   This type of knife is distinguished by its cutting edge, which has very sharp oval grooves or scalloped teeth contoured from grinding. Such blades reduce the friction of slicing and are ideal for cutting foods that are firm on the outside but fragile on the inside. Thin blades are practical for cutting neat slices of tomatoes, fruits, and vegetables, while wide blades are better suited to slicing through cakes, crusty loaves of bread, or pâté en croûte.

• Overlap alternate slices of tomato, red onion, and round mozzarella cheese on a glazed black serving plate. Drizzle verdant pesto sauce over the top of the arrangement. Lightly sprinkle with pignoli (pine nuts).

BONING KNIFE   Obvious in its function, this very sharp, pointed knife is used to remove the bones from poultry and large cuts of meat. Your butcher will generally do any boning you require, but there might be times when you wish to do this job yourself. For example, if whole chickens are on sale you could save a good deal by cutting them up and boning them yourself, instead of buying separate parts. Wings and legs could be used for fricassee or deep frying, boneless breasts for quick sautéing, and the carcass and trimmings for homemade stock.

• Sauté boneless chicken breasts in butter until tender and transfer to a warm plate. Deglaze the pan with ¼ to ½ cup raspberry vinegar. Quickly reheat the chicken breasts, turning them in the sauce. Place the breasts on a large white serving platter and pour the pan juices over. Sprinkle with a handful of fresh raspberries and surround with small bundles of steamed green beans.

FLUTED KNIFE   This stainless steel, sharp, wavy-edged knife with a 4½-inch blade does a beautiful job of fluting, waffle-cutting, or crinkle-cutting all kinds of firm vegetables for salads, french fries, and pickles.

• Use the fluted knife to cut thin decorative slices of raw zucchini, yellow squash, and radishes. Toss with your favorite dressing and serve the colorful salad combination in a clear glass bowl. Sprinkle with chopped chives for added color and flavor.

• Slice cold cooked beets with the fluted knife. Serve the decorative rounds on a bed of watercress and sprinkle with crisp bacon bits.

• Crinkle-cut cubes of melon and use with a combination of seedless green grapes, pitted cherries, and orange sections for an attractive fruit salad. Crinkle-cut cubes of firm cheese could also be mixed in. Serve in the curve of a Boston lettuce leaf placed on a large white plate.

GRAPEFRUIT KNIFE   The slightly curved tip on the flexible serrated blade of this knife is the ideal shape for loosening grapefruit sections or separating the flesh from the rind. The knife works equally well for hollowing all types of rounded fruits and vegetables including citrus fruits, tomatoes, and bell peppers. In addition it is well suited to cutting the fruit away from curved wedges of melon or pineapple.

Fluted Knife

- Slice the top off a bell pepper and hollow the cavity with a grapefruit knife. Stuff with a mixture of cream cheese, minced apple, finely chopped walnuts, and chives. Chill well, then cut crosswise into ½-inch slices, arranging them in an overlapping pattern on a bed of salad greens accompanied by your favorite vinaigrette dressing.

- Cut a cantaloupe crosswise into 1¼-inch slices. Use the rounded ends for another purpose. Remove the seeds and use a grapefruit knife to release the flesh from the rind neatly, leaving the rind intact as a border trim. Place each melon slice on a brightly colored plate and top the inner hollow with a generous scoop of chicken or tuna salad sprinkled with chopped chives and crumbled bacon bits. Set a bright orange gladiolus blossom on the border of each plate.

ZIGZAG or V-KNIFE The folded, double-edged blade of the zigzag knife cuts decorative v-shaped incisions and is generally used to bisect fruits and vegetables. To use, insert the knife halfway through the center of a round fruit, such as a lemon. Retract the blade and reinsert it next to the first incision. Repeat the process all the way around the fruit until it is cut in half in a decorative saw-toothed pattern.

- Place snippets of parsley in the center of jagged-cut lemon halves and use them to adorn a platter of fried fish.

- Allow an older child to use this knife to carve a saw-toothed grin for a Halloween pumpkin.

- Halve cantaloupes with a decorative v-shaped edge. Remove seeds and fill each center cavity with a large scoop of lemon sherbet. Place a sprig of mint leaves between the sherbet and the fruit, and serve the melon on a deep green plate accented with 3 perfect red strawberries.

3.
Setting Pretty

When you set the table you are actually setting the stage for your own production. The ambiance and mood created can be as important to the success of the meal as the food that is served, and caring how your table looks is a way of showing your family and friends how you feel about them. Not long ago it was simple—but not quite so entertaining. Everything matched and a good set of china included every piece you needed to serve a formal sit-down dinner or a buffet. But, with today's limited storage space, inherited odds and ends, informal gatherings and one-course meals, people have taken to improvising with multi-functional items and mixing and matching tableware, whether it be their own, borrowed, or rented. The table top has become a place for individual expression. Traditional settings can be dressed up or down with personal mementos and decorative objects that characterize your individual style and offer imaginative variety.

When all is said and done, it's often the little touches that best project the individual. So use your imagination to let your own special personality come through in your table settings. Don't be afraid to fall in love with unusual items or to use them in unusual ways. If you adore animals, allow your collection of porcelain creatures to adorn your centerpiece some evening. If you love to travel, make that statement with the nostalgia of a railroad set retrieved from the attic; if your table is large enough, you might even use the cars to pass the salt and pepper. Reveal your affinity for nature with a setting of last summer's seashells or autumn's pine cones and acorns. Whatever it is, if you like the idea, try it. If it doesn't work the first time, move things around and keep at it until the look is one you love. Then, and only then, will the look be that special reflection of yourself that you want it to be. The aim is to produce a memorable visual image that will make each meal a special occasion.

*

Table Napery

Inspired settings begin with the napery. Although linen shops offer a wide variety of cloths, mats, and napkins, your choice need not be limited to the selections of conventional outlets. All it takes is a bit of imagination or perhaps some hemming to put any fabric to use.

For instance:

• Tablecloths have two advantages over place mats—you can put more on your table without its appearing cluttered; and you can use a silence cloth or padded mat underneath to protect your table.

• Lace cloths can be laid on a bare table unless you want to use a contrasting color underneath for a special effect.

• A length of wide-wale corduroy in an earth tone can give an appealing textured look to an autumn table.

• A new hand-woven cotton rug can make a spicy contribution to an Indian meal.

• A tartan blanket can add a sporting touch to a buffet laid out for television football fans.

• A thinly padded antique quilt might be just the right touch of Americana for a Fourth of July dinner. Use in combination with place mats if you're nervous about spills.

• A colorful beach towel might be the perfect backdrop on which to display your centerpiece of summer shells or to serve a seafood dinner. Use solid-color hand towels in an appropriate shade for napkins.

• Set your table with a colorful sheet. Use a matching pillowcase to line the outside of a plastic bucket that can be filled with ice in which to chill your beer or wine.

• A paisley or floral peasant shawl makes a colorful table adornment for an ethnic meal.

• Place mats come in a vast assortment of shapes, sizes, colors, and textures—some are fancy and some are plain. When selecting them, choose mats that will harmonize not only with your tableware but also with your room setting. Plan a wardrobe of these to add variety to your table.

• Square dinner napkins laid out in a diamond shape make interesting overlay mats that can extend the service period of a cloth. They can protect the cloth or hide stains from a previous sitting.

• Lacy paper doilies lend themselves as delicate mats for St. Valentine's Day or when serving tea, sandwiches, or dessert.

• Colorful ribbons make a festive adornment over any cloth. Use your centerpiece to anchor a dozen or more ¼-inch-wide satiny pastel ribbons and allow the ends to dangle in soft curls over the edge of the table, streamer fashion. Mix and match the colors—such as violet, pink, and salmon ribbons over a mauve cloth. Coordinate your candles in the same colors, if possible.

• Weave mats or an entire overlay for your cloth out of lengths of sturdy ribbon. Dissimilar widths will make a more interesting pattern. Lay several ribbons about an inch apart in horizontal rows. Vertically weave matching strands in an over-under motion. It is only necessary to weave the center part of the pattern, just enough to hold the mat or overlay together. Allow the tail ends to hang over the edge of the table.

• Tie a pretty bow around a rolled napkin to make a ribbon ring.

• Search secondhand and thrift shops or crochet your own antimacassars. Once used to cover the arms and backs of chairs, some of these are pretty enough to be used on the table.

• Mirrors, framed or unframed, in appropriate sizes and shapes can be used as place mats to contribute double sparkle to your table by causing a splendid ricochet of candlelight and gleaming crystal.

• Let your children have fun making homemade place mats. Cut sheet cork into 12 × 15 inch rectangles. Paint colorful designs or draw bright

With a bit of imagination, a snack or a meal for one person can delight the eye as well as the palate.

WOMAN'S DAY STUDIO

Three table runners are used here, instead of place mats, to create an attractive setting for six (above).

For added eye appeal, present after-dinner coffee in a pretty liqueur-and-green-sugar-rimmed cup; coffee mousse in a delicate porcelain cup; scoops of sherbet sprinkled with freshly grated chocolate in a stemmed crystal bowl (right).

BILL HELMS

IRWIN HOROWITZ

Holidays offer a unique opportunity to really have fun with food. On the Fourth of July, think red, white, and blue (above)!

Festive brunch ideas: Accent a platter of scrambled eggs with diced red pepper; stack warm bagels on long-necked wine bottles (left).

BILL HELMS

WILL ROUSSEAU

Tuck sliced fresh mushrooms between the salad and the bowl or line the bowl with the outside leaves from a head of cabbage or lettuce to lift your salads out of the ordinary.

borders with wax crayons. Or cut felt or canvas into large rectangles or ovals and let the kids decorate these with paints or fabric glue-ons.

• Truly unique place settings can be created by utilizing panes of glass. Arrange flat or pressed leaves and flowers in individual designs directly on top of the table or on a cloth. Place a glass pane over each. This allows total visibility while protecting the arrangement. Be sure to handle the glass with care and mask any rough edges with colored tape.

• Large hand-painted ceramic tiles lend an exotic look to the table. They can be used as individual settings or in place of trivets.

• Palm-frond fans make practical as well as pretty place mats.

• Large wicker or lacquered trays can be used as interesting place settings for an informal meal.

• Dress your table with a layered look. Use a solid-colored medium-length cloth over a multicolored floor-length cloth. Accent the look with matching napkins and/or place mats.

• Jaunty fabrics needn't be restricted to use solely as tablecloths and napkins. Coil a length of fabric turban-style around a wine cooler or ice bucket. This is functional as well as decorative because the cloth absorbs the ice's condensation.

• Loosely braid three long flimsy scarves in matching or harmonizing colors. Rakishly drape the braid around any bowl that needs added pizzazz.

• Table runners may be used instead of place mats for an unusual accent. Position two runners, one on top of the other, in the shape of a cross if you're seating four at a square table. Or position three runners overlapping in a star shape to seat six at a round table. Use your imagination to achieve varied patterns.

• Napkins can either match or contrast with your cloth or mats. If you want to have the most interesting napkins in town, take a course or check a book on napkin folding.

• If you are going to serve food that must be eaten with the hands, such as corn on the cob, spareribs, or fried chicken, set a couple of packets of Wash'n Dri premoistened towelettes on or next to the table napkin. This is a thoughtful gesture used in place of bothersome finger bowls.

- Rustic plaid Irish linen dish toweling doubles as charming napkins.

- Gaily patterned tea towels can be folded in thirds lengthwise, then rolled up and tied with a long thin ribbon. Position on the table as you would a napkin, and place the fork in the center with tines down.

- Terry hand towels can function as either mats or napkins.

- On a buffet table, offer an assortment of solid-colored napkins and allow each diner to choose the color that fits his or her mood.

- Colorful bandanas add a rustic touch when used as napkins.

- Combine pastel floral printed napkins with a solid pastel tablecloth to revitalize a winter-weary table. Mark each place setting with individual spring flowers.

- Let your adolescents or teens make their own stain-resistant table toppers. Cover the surface of a table with interesting clippings from magazines, snapshots, comic strips, or gift wrap and then top them with a sheet of clear heavy plastic taped to the underside of the table. Individual place mats can be made almost the same way: cover one large picture or a collage of clippings laid out on cardboard with clear self-adhesive plastic, following the directions on the backing. For a reversible mat, use two pictures, back to back. Both types of plastic are available through hardware and household-supply stores.

- For a children's party, spread the table with a solid white or pastel-colored vinyl cloth. Use thick felt-tip pens to write each child's name above his setting. It's fun to draw pictures and write messages on the cloth as well. Colorful face cloths make practical and pretty napkins for any children's occasion.

- If you want your guests to feel really special, pin a single camellia corsage to each lady's napkin and a carnation boutonniere to each man's.

- Crochet lacy borders on plain linen napkins and place mats for a uniquely personal setting.

❋

A Guide to Six Attractive, but Simple Napkin Folds

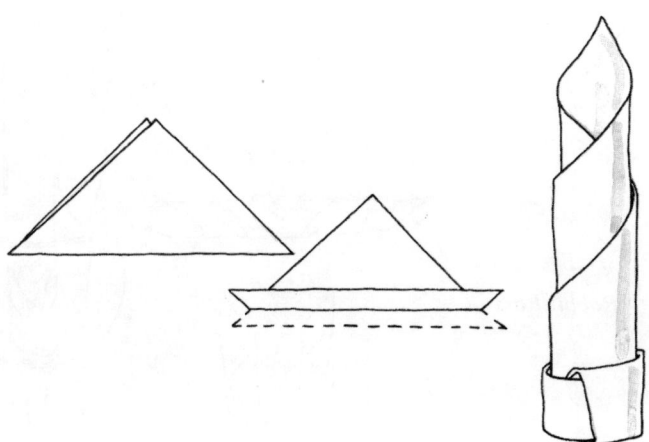

Candle

1. Fold napkin into a large triangle with the open points at top.
2. Fold bottom edge up one inch. Turn napkin over so that the folded edge is face down.
3. Starting at the left side, roll tightly. Tuck loose corner into folds. Stand upright.

Rabbit Ears

1. Lay napkin flat and position on the table like a diamond. Beginning with the bottom corner, roll up the napkin.
2. Place your finger on the napkin point in the center of roll.
3. Holding the point in place, fold the napkin tube in half.
4. Place the folded tube in the hollow of a glass.

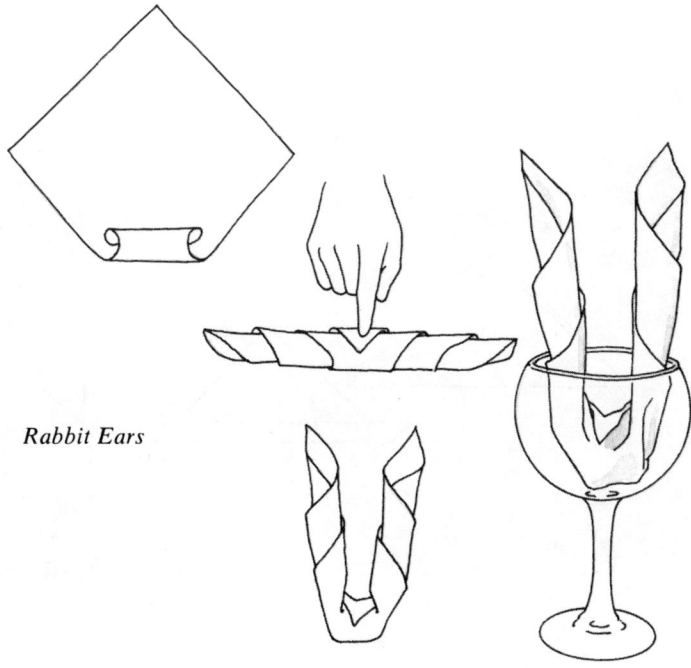

Rabbit Ears

Buffet Server

1. Fold napkin in half and fold again into a square. Lay on the table with the open points at center top.
2. Turn down first free point to opposite corner at center bottom.
3. Turn left and right corners under.
4. Insert flatware in pocket.

Double Diamonds

1. Fold napkin in half and fold again into a square. Lay on table with the open points at center top.
2. Turn down first free point to opposite corner at center bottom.
3. Turn next free corner down to touch the center fold.
4. Fold first corner back to meet second corner at center.
5. Fold left and right corners under.
6. Press with a warm iron to secure folds.

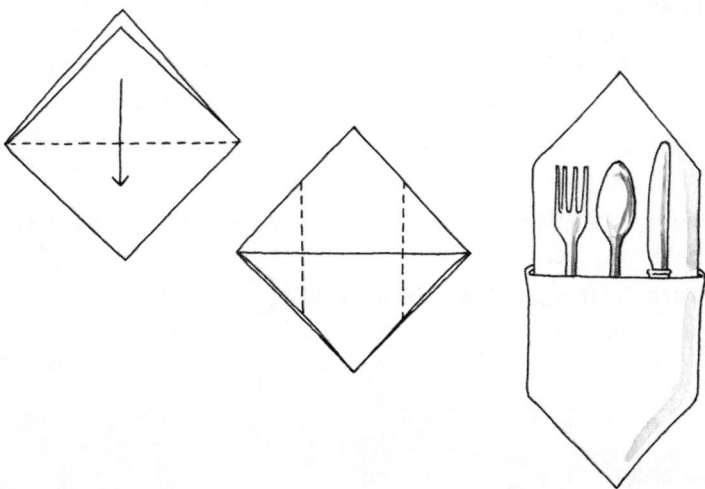

Buffet Server

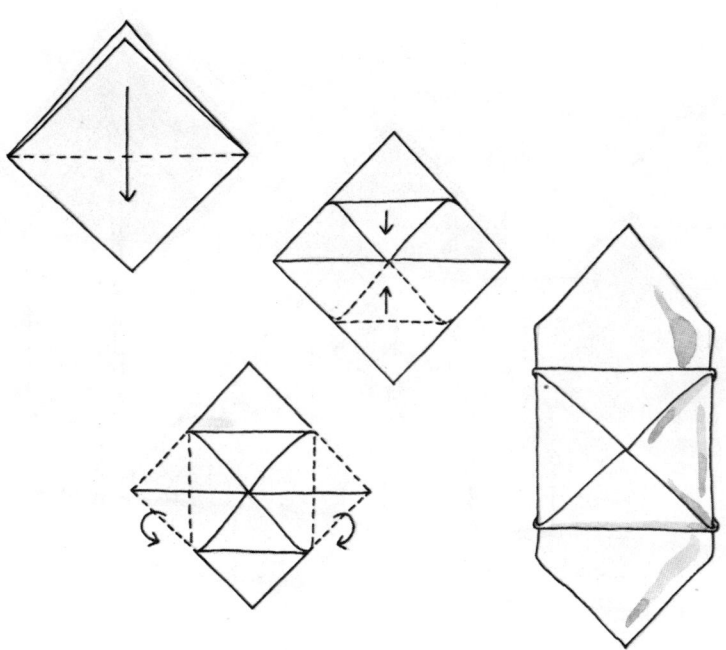

Double Diamonds

Bishop's Hat

1. Fold napkin into a large triangle with the open points at top.
2. Fold the right and left corners up to meet the top corners.
3. Fold up the bottom point to within one inch of the top point.
4. Fold the same point back to the bottom edge.
5. Turn the napkin over. Fold the left side toward the center, and fold the right side over the left.
6. Tuck the free point into the left fold.
7. Stand upright.

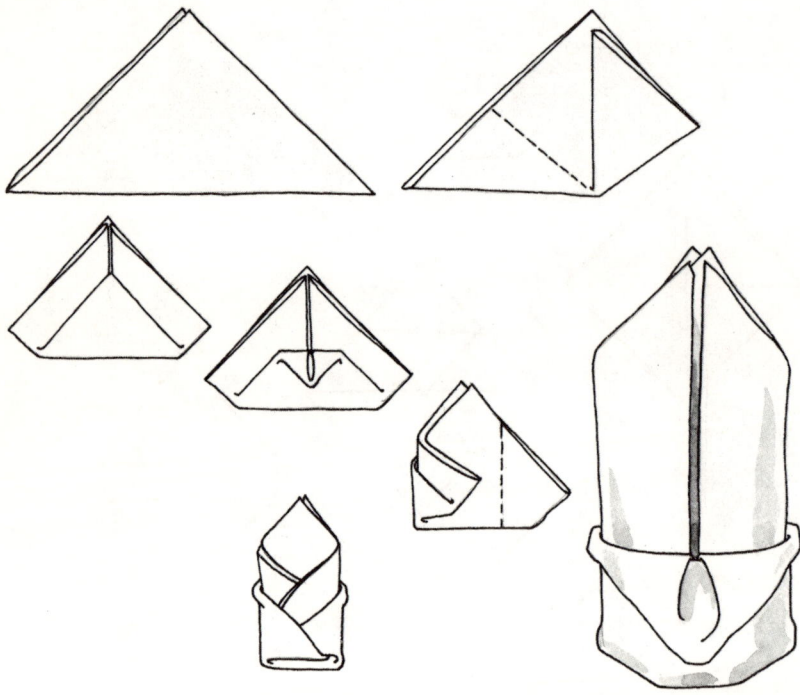

Bishop's Hat

Spanish Fan

1. Fold the napkin in half from top to bottom.
2. Starting at the right side, crease the napkin into 1-inch accordion pleats, leaving the last 4 inches unfolded. Press pleats with a warm iron for sharper edges.
3. Fold the napkin in half, top to bottom, with the pleats on the outside.
4. Fold up the lower left corner and tuck it into the pleats.
5. Invert napkin; stand it on a plate and spread pleats apart.

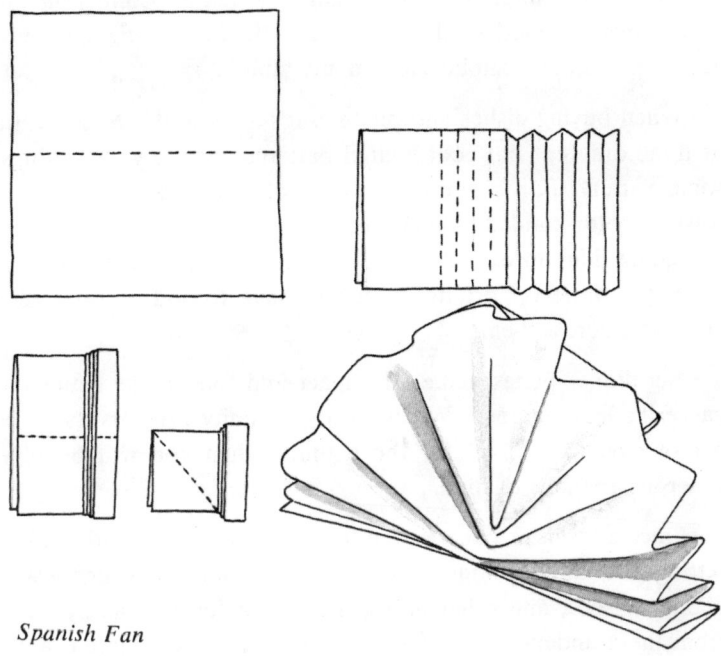

Spanish Fan

Plate Service

Dazzling table settings no longer mean that you have to rush out and buy "service for eight people." These days mixing and matching plate patterns makes the most interesting backdrop at mealtime. What if you only have two sets of dinnerware—one everyday and one formal? Does your choice of table settings narrow down to two? Not at all! Your options are practically endless if you parlay your two sets of dinnerware in varying combinations and prop them with apt accessories. You can deliberately use an interplay of simplicity and elegance to characterize a style and carry out your themes.

• Buy "service for one" whenever you see a pattern that strikes your fancy. Set each place with a different setting and create individual fantasies.

• Watch for open-stock sales, then purchase several dinner plates in a pattern you adore. Accessorize the plates with less expensive solid-color tableware in a harmonizing color.

• Remember simplicity and versatility when selecting your most elegant accessories. A good gold bracelet can be worn with any outfit; a good gold-rimmed bowl can be used on any table.

• When buying dishes and platters, it's a good idea to select them in two or three different but coordinated patterns so that your settings will have some variety. For example, a plain-colored plate accompanied by contrasting color-banded salad dishes or soup bowls is far more stylish and intriguing than an entirely matching service. The more neutral the dinner plate, the more opportunity you will have to add unusual accessories as you come across them.

• Big dinner plates make an impact and food looks better on them because it's less cramped. When the opportunity presents itself, buy a number of oversized plates for those times when you will be serving extra-generous amounts of food.

• Once a week or once a month, maybe on a weekend, make a point of setting the dining-room table formally with all your best silverware, glasses, dishes, and other accessories—just for the family. It's an escape from the mundane, a learning experience for the children, and a celebration for everyone. In this festive environment, children can acquire an appreciation of nice things and learn the basics of good table manners which will give them confidence throughout life.

• Serve your dessert on a dinner plate instead of on a bread-and-butter plate for an impressive change. Accent each serving with a single flower blossom, a daisy, or a sprig of forsythia.

• Use a Frisbee as a holder for a paper plate at a children's party. It's practical during the meal, and makes a great party favor.

• A layered look in plates can be fascinating. Use an oversized dinner plate in the manner of a tray. On it, place a demitasse saucer and cup; a tiny saucedish hugging a scoop of sherbet; and a colorful dessert plate containing a solitary piece of fruit, such as a pear, a nectarine, or a cluster of grapes.

• When selecting a plate pattern, think of the dish as a background that will frame the food you put on it. The edge of the dish is actually more important than the center. Dinnerware can be beautiful on its own, but what counts is the way it will look when in use. Dishes with plain or simple borders are often more effective in food presentation because they act as a frame for your food and do not detract from the color and design of the food itself. A dish with a splashy print border, on the other hand, may clash with the scheme of its contents unless the food is very plain and simple.

Flatware

• The tableware item that's most often taken for granted is flatware. Stainless can be as shiny as sterling, and it comes in a vast assortment of styles and patterns. If you buy interesting knives, forks, and spoons when you see them, it's possible to build a collection of unmatched but harmonious flatware that won't go unnoticed on your table.

• Instead of buying an entire set of matching flatware, purchase "service for one" in several harmonizing patterns.

• Stainless flatware with colored plastic handles lends a decorative touch to the table. Mix and match a quantity of yellow and black handles or build up a set in pretty pastel tones. Pull the whole effect together with matching colored candles.

• Shop around for an unusual pair of small scissors that will look attractive on your table. Use them to snip off small clusters when serving bunch grapes.

• Enlarge your set of flatware with specialized pieces. A collection of fruit knives and forks, for example, might encourage your family to eat more fresh fruit.

• Canapé spreaders can also be used to serve butter or soft cheeses.

• A pair of decorative tongs can serve ice and sugar cubes as well as spaghetti or salad.

• Demitasse spoons can be used to sprinkle salt and pepper from miniature dishes, or they might be just the right size for serving mustard, relish, chutney, cocktail onions, or other condiments.

Centerpiece Ideas

You needn't be having a party in order to put a centerpiece on your table, but having one there will help lend a festive aura to your meals.

Actually, "centerpiece" today has a broader meaning from that of the past when it represented a formal arrangement of flowers placed in the middle of your table. More correctly, it now refers to table decorations of all sorts including fresh, dried, or artificial flowers; plants; fruits and vegetables; candles; knickknacks; or anything else that you might find appropriately interesting. These may be placed anywhere there's room on your table—in the center, at either end, randomly scattered about, or at each place setting.

Improvisation is your best bet, and creating unusual centerpieces can be a fun task that your children can share. For example, an adolescent could lay the table with a large beach towel. A younger child could stage this with a plastic beach bucket filled with daisies, a plastic spade and rake, a few seashells collected from last summer, and a sand sieve lined with a napkin and filled with rolls or sliced bread.

Following are a few more thoughts to help create a pleasant dining atmosphere which will contribute to the enjoyment of your meals:

• Search out unusual containers to hold your decorations. Toys, antique pitchers, soup tureens, baskets, or copper pots, for example, can add interest to your arrangements. Anything that can hold water can be used, as well as some things that can't hold water, like a small bread basket. The secret of waterproofing is to line the container with a foil plate, a shallow bowl, a saucer, or a waxed paper cup if the container is very small.

• Hollowed vegetables have a charm all their own. Halve and seed large bell peppers, then place a small block of florist's foam inside the cavities

Setting Pretty 77

and poke short-stemmed flowers into that. Or stand peppers on end, slice off the top, and remove the seeds for an upright vase. Small pumpkins, pineapples, melons, and grapefruit shells are also suitable. To keep tippy vegetables and fruit level, stick air-dry clay or florist's gum underneath.

• Completely surround a tall plastic tumbler with glued-on candy canes. Tie with a red-checked ribbon. Fill the candy-cane vase with white narcissus.

• Slice the top off a fat butternut squash. Hollow out the insides and fill with water to make a charming vase for a bunch of tiger lilies. Or hollow an acorn squash to be used as a squat container for yellow daisies.

• A collection of 5 or 6 old canning jars can be stuffed with buttercups and Queen Anne's lace. Accent the grouping by placing 2 or 3 lemons on the table next to the jars.

• Coffee, tea, or flowers? Stuff a white enameled teakettle with a bunch of pink tea roses, or arrange a bouquet of yellow and orange mums in a brown and white speckled enameled coffeepot. Place a short-stemmed peony blossom in each of several coffee mugs and scatter them over the table.

• A large goldfish bowl makes an ideal container for 18 long-stemmed carnations, 6 red, 6 pink, and 6 white. Garnish with a few long sprigs of feathery fresh dill.

• A few sprays of forsythia in a garden-sized watering can or a cluster of fragrant lilacs in a shiny metal pail could add charm to an outdoor picnic table.

• A group of beautiful seashells can make a stunning table decoration. To keep tippy shells upright, place a wad of air-dry clay or florist's gum on the bottom side of each shell. Soak a small amount of florist's foam in water, then stuff this into the mouth of each shell. Arrange the shells on your table and poke short-stemmed flowers into the saturated foam. Black-eyed Susans, iris, and ivy are a colorful combination.

• A punch bowl set can create a striking floral presentation. Place 3 gladiolus sprays, 4 carnation stems, and 5 iris bound together with florist's wire into a multipronged metal flower stand in the center of the punch bowl. Partially fill with water, and float additional blossoms in the surrounding pool. Make mini-bouquets in the matching punch cups and set these around the table.

• Many liqueur bottles have graceful shapes and can be recycled for use on your dining table. Delicate long-stemmed flowers, one to each bottle, can be combined with lengths of trailing ivy for a beautiful effect. Wire the ivy with thin florist's wire so that it can be curved into any desired shape.

• Use fresh herbs as part of a flower arrangement. Place nosegays of parlsey and mint in demitasse cups and insert short-stemmed flowers, such as pansies or violets, through the greenery. Place a cup with saucer at each setting.

• Combine 2 leafy bunches of bright red radishes in the center of your table and plant a half dozen perfect tomatoes in between and around them. Stand 3 or 4 white candles within the grouping of red vegetables.

• Fill a glass punch bowl with crushed ice and plunge 3 bunches of trimmed, full-length celery into the center. Nestle 2 bowls of dip on either side of the celery forest. Edge the entire punch bowl with radish roses. Mound the remaining spaces with cherry tomatoes, black olives, raw mushrooms, and red and green pepper sticks.

• Fill a large wooden salad bowl with red apples, pine cones, and bunches of purple grapes. Accent with tall red candles placed around the bowl.

• Place a large crystal bowl on a red tablecloth. Fill with red apples, unshelled almonds, and large prunes.

• Set a wicker tray on a table spread with a Black Watch plaid cloth. Fill with green apples, green grapes, and yellow pears. Dark green napkins and medium green candles would add a memorable touch.

• Fill a green enameled colander with polished red and green apples. Surround it with white votive candles.

• Line a pretty sewing basket with aluminum foil. Fill with nectarines, oranges, purple plums, and clusters of green grapes.

✷

Multifunctional Tableware

Coffeepots are for serving coffee and soup tureens are for serving soup —or are they? With only a bit of imagination, it's possible to put specialized serving dishes and tableware items to fanciful, functional use. Consider these suggestions and go on to find other uses for your various tableware items.

BASKETS   These come in a seemingly infinite variety of shapes, sizes, and weaves. Filled with greenery or edible treats, they add warmth and charm to your table.

• A hamper of juicy oranges and tangerines can be stuck with branches of evergreen and tied with a green plaid bow.

• Line a basket with red and orange tissue paper and fill it with a mound of flawless rosy peaches.

• Line a bread basket with a bright blue and purple bandana. Arrange overlapping pieces of crisply fried chicken and insert slices of green lime throughout.

• Fill a small round basket with fresh raspberries, fill an oval basket with strawberries, and fill a square basket with blueberries. Arrange these on a large woven tray with a pitcher of cream and a sugar bowl.

• Serve a meal in individual baskets that can be carried to your porch, patio, family room, or wherever. Select a large, sturdy rectangular basket, for example. Line it with a red and white checked linen napkin. Place a green bowl filled with tomato and green bean salad in the center of the basket. Arrange a couple of pieces of baked chicken on aluminum foil in one corner, a golden apple cut into wedges in another corner. Spread the apple apart and nest a small slab of blue cheese between the slices. Add a foil-wrapped baked potato to complete the setting.

• Or, in a sturdy, shallow round basket, you could spread a blue and white checked napkin as a colorful background. Set a crock of piping-hot chili con carne in the center. Quarter a grilled cheese sandwich and arrange the triangles in overlapping slices on foil on one side; a salad of small romaine lettuce leaves, cucumber spears, cherry tomatoes, and red onion slices nestled in a plastic bag on another side. Place a ramekin of baked orange custard on a tray for dessert. Include a knife, fork, and spoon, small salt and pepper shakers, several paper napkins, and a packaged moist towel tucked into the tray arrangement.

• For basket improvisation, invert a straw hat such as a sombrero and fill the cavity with a potted plant.

BOTTLES You can recycle bottles for use on your table instead of throwing them away. Champagne bottles, wine bottles, mineral water bottles, liqueur bottles, and even some soda bottles are attractive enough to make interesting containers once the labels are soaked off. Try them as:

• candleholders

• containers for chilled tap water

• vases for long-stemmed flowers; for an unusual arrangement, group several bottles together, each holding a different flower

• containers for iced tea, iced coffee, punch, sangría, or lemonade

• decanters to replace the unattractive milk carton

BOWLS Large or small, these receptacles have limitless uses in the kitchen as well as on the dining table. Rice bowls, for example, can add flair and color to your table in many unexpected ways. They come in decorative geometric or oriental patterns that are more fun to mix than to match, as long as the colors harmonize.

• They are a perfect shape for serving grapefruit.

• They are an ideal size to be used as condiment containers. They can hold mustard, relish, chutney, ketchup, jams, or jellies, replacing unsightly jars and bottles.

• Use them in place of soup bowls for added variety.

• They make decorative bowls for serving ice cream, fruit cups, puddings, or other desserts.

• When you're not serving rice, let them hold individual portions of sauced vegetables, spaghetti, chili con carne, or cereal.

• Present your family with a do-it-yourself salad bar. Place a large bowl of salad greens in the center of your table. Circle it with rice bowls containing a selection of salad fixings: grated cheese, bacon bits, cherry tomatoes, chopped onion, cucumber slices, sliced pickled beets, drained garbanzo beans, croutons.

• Use rice bowls as serving containers for artichokes. Set a colorful rice bowl on a large dinner plate, which can be used to hold the discarded artichoke leaves. Add a second rice bowl containing the dip for the artichokes.

• Use as finger bowls—fill each bowl halfway with warm water and float a few flower petals on the surface or garnish with a lemon slice. These make a delightful surprise when served with everyday finger foods such as fried chicken, spareribs, and corn on the cob, as well as special-occasion lobster or crab.

• Float a flower blossom in each rice bowl and arrange the bowls as a centerpiece in the middle of your table or as individual decorations for each place setting.

• Soup bowls, too, have uses other than for the obvious liquid. They can hold portions of spaghetti, stew, or salad as well as fill any of the functions appropriate for rice bowls.

• Owning a large glass bowl can be a tremendous asset for colorful food presentation.

• Serve a mouth-watering layered fruit salad resembling a rainbow in your glass bowl. Start with marbles of seedless green grapes, then top with fruits in order: wedges of nectarines, cubes of watermelon, purple plum halves, orange sections, and sliced kiwi.

• Present a salad in colorful layers: shredded lettuce, cherry tomatoes, steamed and cooled green beans, steamed and cooled cauliflowerets and alfalfa sprouts.

• Use it as a tureen to serve a cold, colorful gazpacho with cubed cucumber, tomatoes, green peppers, and croutons.

• Entice your diners with a tortellini salad studded with colorful capers, black olives, diced red pepper, and snippets of fresh dill and basil leaves, displayed in a glass bowl.

• Drape a red, white, and blue napkin inside the bowl and fill it with a mound of homemade rolls and buns. Poke bread sticks in between the buns for added dimension.

• Fill a glass bowl with apples, oranges, dates, dried figs, and unshelled walnuts and almonds. Hang nutcrackers around the edge of the bowl.

CAKE PLATE   Remove the restrictions on this large round plate and you can find many uses for it:

• Pies, tarts, cupcakes, pastries, cheese, and pizza can all be presented on a cake plate.

• Arrange whole fruits, pears, peaches, grapes, and bananas into an edible centerpiece. Stud the arrangement with beautiful red Bing cherries.

• Arrange 2 golden delicious apples and a bunch of seedless green grapes next to a generous wedge of oozing Brie on a cake plate made of blue milk glass.

• Present a steaming meat loaf on a pedestal cake plate. Surround it with boiled red-skinned potatoes and alternating bunches of cauliflower and broccoli flowerets.

• Unmold a shiny purple Greek moussaka on a stainless steel cake plate. Tuck sprigs of watercress all around the edges, and place cherry tomatoes 2 inches apart in the greenery. Serve with tomato sauce on the side in a stainless steel boat.

• Set a round fruitcake on a crystal cake stand and surround it with a garland of trailing cedar. Top cake with candied red and green cherries and pecan halves.

Setting Pretty 83

CARAFES These gracefully shaped pouring vessels, large and small, can be put to many uses other than holding wine:

• They can hold any kind of chilled drink, such as milk, iced tea, iced coffee, sangría, fruit drinks, fruit juice, cocktails, or beef bouillon.

• Use them to dispense straws.

• A wide-mouthed carafe makes a charming container for bread sticks.

• Peppermint or licorice sticks could be served in a carafe.

• A carafe is just the right size to be used as a vase for a bunch of anemones. Tie it with a green striped bow for added flair.

CHAFING DISH Use this as a container for a centerpiece arrangement of red-skinned onions, green peppers, and daisies, or be practical and use it to serve fondue, stew, soup, paella, or a piping-hot casserole of chicken, corn, diced peppers, and tomatoes.

COFFEE AND TEA ACCOUTERMENTS Pots, cups, and mugs can be used interchangeably to break a habitual routine. Try serving tea in your coffeepot, hot chocolate or coffee in your teapot.

• Coffee- and teapots also make charming dispensers for hot soup or consommé that can be drunk in matching cups.

• Hot clam broth in a teapot poured into teacups makes an unusual accompaniment to steamed clams.

• Freshen spirits on a hot summer afternoon by serving iced tea in your silver coffee service.

Demitasse cups and saucers can be very versatile:

• Fill the cups halfway with crushed ice; use as individual containers for butter curls with the saucer serving as a plate for a bread stick and a couple of crackers.

• Use the cups as containers for chocolate sauce or other dessert sauces; surround the cup with whole strawberries or other small fruits, chunks of poundcake, or marshmallows for dunking.

• Use as melted butter containers when serving lobsters or hot artichokes. Vinaigrette may be served in the cup for cold artichokes.

• Place mini-bouquets of wild flowers and grass in the cups and arrange them around the table at each place setting.

• Fill the cups with your favorite dip; surround with small raw vegetables such as mushrooms, radishes, zucchini slices, and cherry tomatoes. Stand a few red and green bell pepper strips and carrot sticks in the cup containing the dip. Serve as an individual first course or afternoon snack.

• Use demitasse saucers as individual salt and pepper containers in a pinch. Hold a table knife, cutting edge down, across the center of the saucer. The knife will serve as a guideline. Sprinkle half the saucer with salt, the other half with black pepper.

• Serve warmed sake (rice wine) in demitasse cups.

• Bake and serve cappuccino soufflés in ovenproof earthenware coffee mugs.

• Prepare a recipe for mocha or coffee mousse and spoon the gelatin mixture into fine bone china coffee cups. Leave a ½-inch space at the top of the cup to hold a garnish of whipped cream sprinkled with instant coffee flakes. Chill the mousse until set, then serve the cups on matching saucers.

COLANDER Normally this item is kept behind the scenes for meal preparation only. However, some colanders are pretty enough to be brought to the table.

• Nest a dozen brown and a half dozen white hard-cooked eggs in a copper colander for a breakfast centerpiece or picnic brunch.

• Pile a white and black speckled enamel colander full of purple plums and baby aubergines.

• Consider the beauty of an orange plastic colander lined with a brown and white striped napkin and nestled with hot rolls.

• For breakfast, set out a colander full of individual boxes of cereal, variety packs of Raisin Bran, Cheerios, Corn Chex, etc., so each family member can choose his or her own.

COOKIE JAR If your cookie jar is made of heat-resistant glass or earthenware, then you have in your possession a serving dish that you were unaware of. Use it at the table to present stews, hot soups, or chili con carne. The large covered jar also makes an ideal container for poached fruit, pickles, or coleslaw for a crowd. And for flowers, try a bunch of red tulips in a cookie jar that resembles a giant strawberry or a bunch of white lilacs in a jar that resembles a huge red apple.

CUTTING BOARD   These attractive wooden slabs are meant for cutting and slicing foods, but there's no reason why a handsome board shouldn't be brought to the table. Use yours to serve bread, cheese, pâté, cold cuts, meat, poultry, or fruit.

• Tie two stems of yellow mums together with a pretty orange checked ribbon. Lay the tied flowers across the cutting board. Stand five nectarines on one side of the flowers, and place a crumbly, creamy wedge of Stilton on the other.

• Set an unmolded pâté in the center of your cutting board. Line overlapping slices of French bread along one side of the pâté. Make a row of cornichons (small pickles) ¼ inch apart along the other side. Place a small crock of golden-yellow mustard at one corner of the board.

• Line a cutting board with long sprigs of feathery dill leaves. Top with a whole baked fish. Arrange overlapping slices of lemon along the top of the fish.

• Remove the silk from the green leaves of freshly shucked corn. Lay the leaves across a wooden cutting board and use as a serving bed for the steamed corn on the cob.

• Wooden cutting boards make handsome trivets—serve bacon-flecked chestnuts and brussels sprouts in a red enameled iron pan set atop a small round board.

EGG CUPS   The small cavity of an egg cup offers an ideal way to present individual servings of:

    butter, melted or packed cold

    dips for vegetables, fruits, or chips

    salad dressings or vinaigrette

    dessert sauces; set a cup of chocolate sauce in the center of a plate containing an unpeeled banana and a small fruit knife and fork

STUFFED-EGG PLATE A serving plate with oval indentations to keep wobbly or slippery stuffed-egg halves from sliding about can be used for other foods as well:

   stuffed mushrooms

   snails surrounded by garlic butter

   cherry tomatoes stuffed with salmon or cream cheese

   clams on the half shell

   clams casino

   stuffed mussels

   stuffed dates

   chocolate bonbons

   whole strawberries

   small clusters of grapes

GLASSES Beyond the classic tumbler, glasses are fashioned in many shapes that can be put to practical use. Goblet-style wineglasses are perhaps the most versatile, the bigger the better.

• Large wine goblets and balloon brandy snifters offer an ideal shape for serving:

   seafood salad; shrimp can be hooked over the rim of the glass

   layered fruit cups; alternate layers of blueberries, melon balls, raspberries, and diced peaches; add a splash of Champagne or off-dry white wine for added effect

   delicate cold puddings, such as lemon mousse topped with raspberries

   parfaits, such as a poached peach half topped with a scoop of coconut ice cream and sauced with puréed raspberries; garnish with a sprig of mint for added color

   desserts, such as strawberry shortcake; line the glass with lady fingers, then fill it with sliced strawberries and top with a swirl of whipped cream; hook an orange slice over the rim of the glass

   chilled soups for sipping; chilled tomato and orange bisque, garnished with a slice of orange and a cherry tomato; or chilled cream of garden pea soup garnished with a swizzle stick of celery

   candy, such as after-dinner mints or jelly beans

• Large goblet-shaped wineglasses can also be used to serve cappuccino or Irish coffee. Place a spoon in the glass before pouring in the hot coffee so that it does not crack. Top with a huge gob of whipped cream sprinkled with instant coffee flakes or mini-chocolate chips.

• Cordial glasses, so very tiny, may double as holders for toothpicks, cigarettes, or tiny bouquets of baby violets and wild flowers.

• Pilsner glasses, tall and v-shaped, lend an attractive appearance to iced tea, iced coffee, gelatin desserts, or flowers.

• Tall glasses are ideal for sipping cold consommé or bouillon. Place a fat straw in the glass and insert a gladiolus blossom (which is removed before sipping!) in the straw. Hook a lemon or lime slice over the rim of the glass.

ICE BUCKET OR WINE COOLER   The tall, fat bucket shape can lend itself to versatile table service very easily:

• Stand 3 or 4 long baguettes (thin loaves of French bread) in a stainless steel ice bucket and tie a yellow and red plaid ribbon around the bucket. Add a few stalks of sea oats (obtainable in a flower shop) for a very pretty picture.

• Wind an Indian-style turban of purple, red, and gold fabric around the base of a crystal wine cooler. This will catch the dripping condensation as well as add a decorative splash of color to your table.

• An insulated ice bucket makes a practical tureen for chilled soup on a summer day. In order to change the look of the bucket, tie a piece of pretty fabric around it and secure with a matching ribbon.

• Place a bunch of fall leaves, red, orange, and gold, in a wooden ice bucket. Surround it with colorful gourds for a beautiful fall centerpiece.

• Line an ice bucket with a red checked linen towel and fill with deep-fried chicken parts for a help-yourself buffet.

• Line an ice bucket with a striped terry hand towel. Stand as many ears of corn upright as will fit.

PITCHERS   The graceful shape of a pitcher with an inviting handle can do much to improve the looks of a table.

• Decant milk or orange or grapefruit juice into an attractive pitcher instead of serving in a cardboard carton. Cover the mouth with plastic wrap for storage in the refrigerator.

• Place a bunch of black-eyed Susans in a white pitcher and stand it on a white dinner plate in the center of your table. Surround the pitcher with lemons and sprigs of mint for added color and aroma.

• Decant jug wine into a pitcher. The presentation will be more attractive and the pitcher will be easier to handle.

• Stand long bread sticks in a decorative pitcher. Tie a ribbon that matches your cloth or place mats to the handle.

PLATTERS Usually used to hold a roast, these oversized plates are excellent for serving hors d'oeuvre, sandwiches, fruit, or individual pies, tarts, and cookies for a crowd. But they don't necessarily have to be reserved only for large gatherings. They make wonderful plates for foods that are messy or difficult to eat. Like spaghetti served with chicken or pork chops, for example, or whole steamed lobsters. Use them instead of dinner plates with those foods that require maneuvering or room to eat.

PUNCH BOWL SET Punch may go in and out of fashion from time to time, but the large bowl and matching cups can be put to use in many different ways.

• Use the bowl as a tureen for chilled soup; serve the soup in the matching cups.

• When serving lobster, use the bowl as a container for the discarded shells; use cups to hold melted butter.

• When serving steamed clams, present them in the bowl, ladle them into large plates, and use the empty bowl for the discarded shells. The cups can hold the clam broth or melted butter.

• Serve salad for a crowd in a punch bowl; cups can hold dressing.

• Fill the bowl and cups part way with water and float opened rose blossoms on the water's surface. Arrange the cups around the bowl or set them at each place.

• Place a generous layer of ice cubes in the bottom of the bowl and pile it with radish roses. Serve a curried dip in the cups.

• Place a generous layer of ice cubes in the bottom of the bowl and top with whole peaches, nectarines, and plums. Make small bouquets of violets in the matching cups that will accent the purple fruit.

SCALLOP SHELLS   What better way to serve seafood than in an attractive container provided by nature? Porcelain scallop shells or natural seashells of various shapes and sizes can add functional beauty to your table.

• Bake and serve scallops in the classic style of coquilles St. Jacques. Pipe a decorative border of mashed potatoes around the edge of the shell after filling it with the mixture of scallops and mushrooms in a cheese sauce. Frozen peas and small shrimp can be mixed in before baking to give added color and texture.

• Bake and serve individual portions of tuna casserole in large scallop shells. Sprinkle with minced parsley and serve on a yellow plate garnished with black olives.

• Bake and serve individual portions of vegetables au gratin in large scallop shells. Dust with sweet paprika and serve on a red plate.

• Fill a baking dish with crushed ice and place large scallop or clamshells on top. Fill with scallop or fish mousse. The ice will keep the shells from tipping and also speed up the chilling time. Once set, garnish with the following: a thin slice of lime topped with half a teaspoon of red caviar, or a thin slice of lemon topped with half a teaspoon of black caviar. Insert snippets of fresh dill under the citrus slices for added color.

• Place a small Boston lettuce leaf in a large scallop shell. Fill with tuna, lobster, or fish salad. Garnish with wedges of sliced hard-cooked egg, small black olives, and capers.

• Serve scallops ceviche (raw marinated scallops) in large scallop shells. Stir small melon balls into the mixture for added flavor and visual appeal.

• Large scallop shells also make marvelous molds for flaky pastry. Roll out the dough, lay the pastry over the outside of one shell and trim the edges. Fit a slightly larger shell over it, sandwich fashion, and bake until golden brown. The pastry will brown beautifully and the fluting will be crisp and detailed. Unmold and fill each pastry shell with curried shrimp sprinkled with shreds of freshly grated coconut.

• Serve shrimp cocktail in large scallop shells. Make a nest of shredded iceberg lettuce in the bottom of each shell cavity. Arrange the shrimp in the shape of an arc around the edge of the shell (tail end pointing outward) and place a mound of cocktail sauce in the center. Sprinkle the sauce with finely shredded lemon zest. Place the shell on a large white dinner plate together with a lemon half stuck with a cocktail fork.

• Arrange deep-fried fish fillets on a serving platter and surround them with individual portions of tartar sauce served in small clamshells. Tuck small bunches of parsley between the shells and arrange overlapping slices of lemon on top of the fish.

SUGAR BOWL AND CREAMER   Pair these together or use them individually as containers for:

• candies or nuts

• dip

• olives, pickles, or cocktail onions

• chutney, relish, or mustard

• jam or honey

• gravy or sauce, such as hollandaise, apple, or horseradish

• sour cream in the creamer; chopped chives in the sugar bowl

• syrups, such as maple, hot fudge, or blueberry syrup

• grated cheese

• raisins to sprinkle on cereal

• small flower arrangement

• melted butter

TUREEN   Aside from being used to serve soup at the table, this deep bowl can also be used as a container for:

- goulash, stew, beef Bourguignonne, chicken fricassee, or coq au vin
- chili con carne
- punch or sangría
- popcorn laced with melted butter
- spaghetti for a crowd
- tossed salad
- poached fruit or fruit compote
- a potted plant (place the pot in the tureen)
- a homemade flower arrangement of daffodils, white tulips, and forsythia

4.
Foods, Plain and Fancy

When people think of decorative foods, garnishes come to mind first. Indeed, they play a major role in food presentations and should be included in every cook's repertoire. However, creating an attractive dish does not lie solely in the realm of sculpted radishes and fan-tailed gherkins. Presenting food is actually very much like arranging flowers. You can take whatever food you are serving and simply heap it on a plate just as you would take a handful of freshly picked flowers and just plunk the entire bunch into a vase. Or, preferably, you can take an appraising look at what you intend to serve and consider how it would best appear on the specific plate you have purposefully selected for that meal. The food should be placed on the dish with an eye toward color and visual balance just as you would select flowers individually and place them in a container to get a desired effect.

Simplicity is the key to attractive food arrangements, and "Less is more" is an ideal motto. The trend today is toward lighter, healthier, smaller portions. The cluttered plate has seen better days. If you feel the need to serve large quantities of food, you can express a lighter style in the way you make your presentation. You don't have to put everything on the plate at the same time. Arrange smaller but attractive portions on each plate and allow those who wish to take second helpings. Otherwise, you might consider buying a set of oversized dishes so that the larger portions of "one serving only" appear to be less cramped.

In addition to the way food is laid out on a plate, the way it's prepared can also lend itself to a more attractive presentation. A new seasoning can add excitement, such as ground cinnamon sprinkled on oatmeal or nutmeg dusted over brussels sprouts. A different napkin in the bread basket can make the bread something new—try a bright yellow and black bandana in an orange plastic basket to perk up your breakfast table. Restyle some of your favorite vegetables simply by changing the cut. Beets, for example, can be diced, sliced, halved, or julienned. Each shape gives a different texture and appearance to the deep red color.

Many examples follow in this chapter, and you will find numerous ways of being creative in the kitchen when handling your food and beverages. These suggestions are not recipes but they should stimulate you to build upon and apply them to your individual life style.

Bread

• To serve bagels, slip them on a long-necked wine bottle, such as one that held Burgundy or Champagne.

• Pile seeded rolls in a copper colander.

• Fill a covered cookie jar with warmed rolls for dinner.

Butter or Margarine

• Pack softened butter into pretty ceramic egg cups which can be used for individual servings.

• Smooth the surface of butter packed into a small crock or egg cup with a warm spatula or knife; then use a dinner fork to draw decorative squiggly lines through the center of the butter.

• Slice ¼-inch pats from a stick of butter. Arrange the slices overlapping on top of each other like felled dominoes.

• Flavored butters flecked with colorful pinpoints of herbs, spices, and seasonings are a world unto themselves. They freeze well and, if packaged in small amounts, will always be on hand to turn a humdrum meal into something special. Pack the flavored butter into a small crock and cover with plastic wrap, or roll it into a cylinder and wrap it in waxed paper. Use to adorn carrots or string beans, a grilled steak or red snapper, or a big bowl of egg noodles. Suggestions for flavoring butter follow:

• HERB BUTTERS Combine softened butter with fresh minced herbs like parsley, chives, dill, etc., and pepper to taste. Add a dash of lemon juice or vermouth for a refreshing flavor.

• SAVORY BUTTERS Try mixing one of these into softened butter: minced shallots, garlic, or onions, green peppercorns, mustard, horseradish, grated Parmesan or cheddar cheese, freshly ground pepper and grated lemon rind, mild paprika, or curry powder.

• VEGETABLE BUTTERS Stir softened butter together with coarsely mashed avocado, finely diced bell peppers, minced fresh or canned pimientos, tomato paste, or finely chopped watercress. Season to taste with herbs and spices if desired.

• BREAKFAST OR DESSERT BUTTERS With an electric mixer, beat softened butter until smooth. Gradually beat in up to, but not more than, an equal quantity of heavy cream. Then let your imagination go wild, or add one or more of the following: a tablespoon or two of strawberry jam and a few crushed fresh strawberries; honey; maple syrup; finely grated orange rind; a whisper of cinnamon; crystallized ginger; grated semi-sweet chocolate; finely shredded coconut. Add a splash of your favorite liqueur, brandy, or rum, if desired. Spread these sweetened butters on toast, bread, or waffles, smear on English muffins, or use to fill crêpes.

• CANAPÉ BUTTERS Combine any of the following with softened butter: mashed liverwurst and a dash of brandy; sieved hard-cooked egg; mashed sardines or tuna; chopped capers seasoned with a few drops of Worcestershire sauce; chopped smoked oysters; blue cheese; caviar. Chili sauce, hot pepper sauce, or lemon juice may also be added for increased flavor.

• SNACK BUTTERS Try blending these with softened butter: finely chopped toasted blanched almonds or pecans together with a few tablespoons of honey; peanut butter; defrosted undiluted fruit juice concentrates; finely minced dried fruits such as apricots, prunes, raisins, or dates.

Foods, Plain and Fancy

- RED WINE BUTTER   Reduce 1 cup of red wine to 1 tablespoon and cool. Blend together with 1 stick of softened butter and 1 finely minced shallot. Serve over meats or vegetables, or use to enrich a meat gravy.

- FLOWER BUTTERS   These make a surprising but delightful addition to any meal. Blend chopped flower petals into softened butter; refrigerate for several hours so that the flavors come out. Spread the flower butter on a sheet of waxed paper, then cut petal shapes and other decorative designs with cookie or aspic cutters. Arrange the cutouts to resemble a flower and chill until serving time. Not all flowers are edible, but these are among those that are suitable: carnations, marigolds, chrysanthemums, dandelions, geraniums, gladioli, violets, honeysuckle, lavender, lilacs, nasturtiums, pansies, roses, and tulips.

- For a mound of butter, pack into an ice cream scoop and chill until firm. Unmold onto a pretty plate or a bread board.

- For an elegant meal, pack butter into small crystal fruit bowls or crystal punch cups.

- Serve scoops of snack butters with popsicle stick spreaders at a children's party. Accompany with plenty of sturdy crackers, toast, or English muffins.

Cakes

"Let them eat cake!" Smaller portions are the rule rather than the exception in today's calorie-conscious society. Try one of these "short" cuts the next time you serve cake. Use a long serrated knife; if the frosting sticks, dip the blade in hot water and wipe with a damp paper towel after each cut.

1. To slice a layer cake into 20 pieces, cut circle as shown. Then cut cake into quarters, and cut each outer quarter into four slices. 2. Or, to cut a layer cake into 28 pieces, cut cake into quarters. Then cut quarters into slices as shown. Only the center pieces can be cut in half.

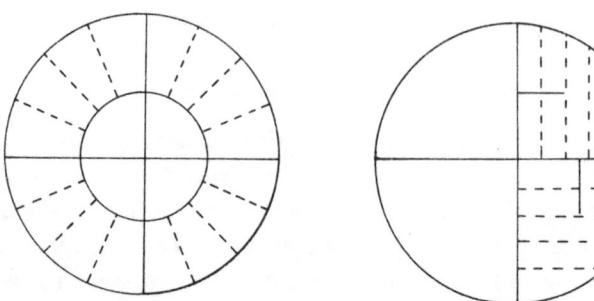

3. To cut an 8-inch square cake into 16 pieces, cut cake into quarters. Then cut diagonally into triangles. 4. To cut a 9-inch square cake into 18 pieces, cut lengthwise and crosswise into thirds. Then cut diagonally into triangles.

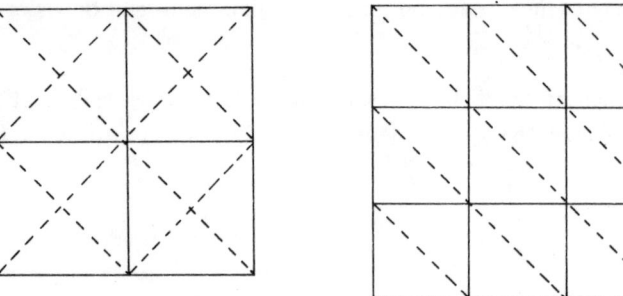

5. To cut a 9 × 13 inch cake into 21 pieces, first cut lengthwise into thirds. Then cut diagonally into parallelograms and triangles. 6. To cut a 9 × 13 inch cake into 24 pieces, cut lengthwise into thirds and crosswise into fourths. Then cut diagonally into triangles.

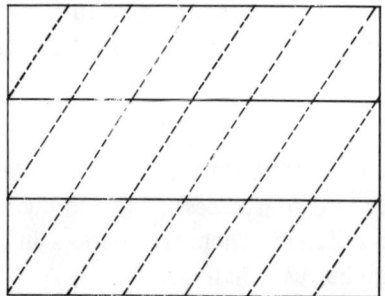
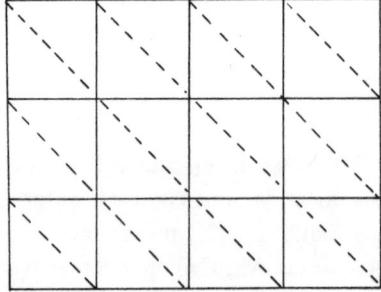

Casseroles

A casserole is often part of a buffet meal or it may be the main dish of a dinner. Most are made with inexpensive ingredients, but you can make them look like a million dollars with attractive garnishes:

• Crunchy toppings that are tasty and quick can be made simply from crumbs which are sprinkled over the top. Make them from crushed cereal like cornflakes, from flavored crackers like whole wheat wafers, or from crushed toasted rye or pumpernickel bread.

• Some casseroles—those made from vegetables, for example—may be garnished with grated cheese, such as Gruyère, mozzarella, Parmesan, or Romano.

• Sliced rounds of green or red bell peppers make a colorful as well as tasty garnish.

• Pastry cutouts go well with many types of casserole. Fancy shapes can be cut with a sharp knife or cookie cutter. Arrange these on top of a casserole—for instance, a circle of spades and clubs—brush the tops with milk, and bake the pastry shapes at the same time as the casserole.

• Cutouts from thin slices of cheese can be placed on a casserole 5 minutes before it is finished baking or as soon as it comes out of the oven. The heat from the casserole will be enough to melt the cheese slightly.

Chocolate

• Fill oversized wine goblets a third full with luscious raspberries. Cap with vanilla-scented sweetened whipped cream. Sprinkle with a spoonful of freshly grated semi-sweet chocolate.

• Serve ice cream or sherbet in your prettiest dessert dishes, and set out a crystal bowl of grated semi-sweet chocolate to sprinkle over the top of each serving. Frosty peppermint ice cream or fruity orange, lemon, or raspberry sherbet combine especially well with chocolate.

• Too busy to make dessert? Buy an assortment of fine handmade chocolates. Remove any candy papers and set the confections on a doily-covered cake plate to be passed around with coffee.

- To grate: Chocolate must be cool and firm. Use a hand grater or a hand-cranked rotary grater. Brush surface frequently to prevent holes from clogging.

- To curl: Chocolate must be slightly warm. Use a swivel-action vegetable peeler. Draw the blade along the surface of a chunk or bar of chocolate. For small curls, pull blade along the narrow side of the chocolate; for large curls, pull blade over the wider surface.

- Warm everyone's heart with a chocolate sherry fondue. In the container of a blender combine: 4 squares unsweetened chocolate, cut into small pieces; 1 cup granulated sugar; ⅔ cup California sherry, heated almost to boiling; 1 teaspoon vanilla extract; 1 tablespoon butter. Blend at high speed until smooth. Transfer to a fondue pot; keep warm over low heat (sauce thickens as it stands). Yield: about 1½ cups. To make ahead: refrigerate and reheat slowly over hot water in a double boiler.

Accompany fondue with fresh fruit cut into bite-size pieces (bananas, apples, oranges, strawberries, seedless grapes) to be dipped in the chocolate. Use your imagination to arrange a colorful fruit platter. Also delectable with this fondue: marshmallows, chunks of poundcake, and plain or spiced doughnuts.

- For a truly dark chocolate cake, lightly dust the cake pans with cocoa instead of flour.

- A pinch of nutmeg will heighten the flavor of your chocolate desserts. Stir it into hot sauce, cake batter, or soufflé mixture before baking.

- Whenever you serve sweetened whipped cream, whether it be with desserts, fruits, coffee, or cocoa, sprinkle a little grated semi-sweet chocolate over the snowy peaks.

- CHOCOLATE LEAVES   Melt 8 ounces semi-sweet chocolate and 1 tablespoon vegetable shortening in top of a double boiler. Using a spoon, generously coat *underside* of camellia or other waxy-type leaves. Chill or freeze until firm. Separate chocolate from leaves, starting at stem end of leaf. Discard leaves. Arrange chocolate leaves on top of cakes, pies, or other desserts.

※

Coffee

• Today we seldom have time for a formal coffee ritual, but an elegant silver-plated or bone china coffeepot can make even a "break" special.

• Serve cappuccino at home for an unusual treat. Combine equal quantities of freshly brewed coffee and steaming-hot milk. Pour into mugs and sprinkle with cinnamon or nutmeg. Or top with whipped cream and a pinch of grated orange zest.

• Spice up your after-dinner coffee. For 2 servings, heat 1¾ cups water in a saucepan with a 1-inch stick of cinnamon, 6 whole cloves, and 5 allspice berries. Bring to a boil and simmer gently for 10 minutes. Strain the water and use it with 2 teaspoons of instant coffee. Or use this water to brew 2 cups of coffee in a coffee machine.

• For a special treat, serve whipped cream with your coffee instead of milk or liquid cream.

• Coffee and liqueur? Sprinkle one saucer with granulated sugar and pour a small amount of green crème de menthe or Sambucca into another saucer. Dip the rim of a demitasse cup into the liqueur and then into the sugar. Repeat the liqueur-sugar dip until a thick coating has built up around the edge of the cup. Fill the prepared cups with espresso and serve with a strip of lemon peel on the saucer.

• Delight coffee drinkers by serving granulated brown sugar in one bowl and granulated white sugar in another. The offer of a choice should surprise them.

• On a very hot day, balance a scoop of coffee, vanilla, or chocolate ice cream on the rim of a tall glass filled two thirds of the way with iced coffee. Serve with a long spoon and a straw.

• Serve iced coffee with frozen coffee cubes.

• Mix 1 part instant coffee powder with 2 parts granulated sugar and sprinkle on hot French toast for breakfast. Or sprinkle the mixture on cookies, hot from the oven.

• Add a pinch of instant coffee powder to meat gravy to improve the color and add a new flavor dimension.

Condiments

Bottles and jars holding ketchup, mustard, relish, pickles, jams, jellies, and honey are familiar accessories on many tables. Why not dress them up?

• Soaking the labels off will immediately improve the appearance of most condiment containers, and in general the shape of the bottle is enough to indicate what's inside. If having unlabeled bottles bothers you, ask your children to design new labels that can be glued on.

• Transfer condiments to more attractive containers, such as extra sugar bowls or creamers, crocks, crystal dishes, or coffee mugs. Place these on a saucer with a spoon so that they will be easy to serve.

Fish

• Overlap thinly sliced lemon rounds in an arc on one side of a large white plate. Arrange 3 thin slices of smoked salmon in front of the lemon and sprinkle them with 2 tablespoons of tiny capers. Complete the picture with a perfect yellow lemon wedge.

• Spread very thin slices of smoked salmon with caper-studded cream cheese and roll up like a jelly roll. Cut the rolls into ½-inch slices. Place a whole, small romaine lettuce leaf in the center of a dinner plate and place 5 salmon rounds in a line down the center of the leaf. Garnish with a lemon wedge.

• Arrange 5 Belgian endive leaves in a star pattern on a red dinner plate. Unmold an individual-sized can of tuna in the center of the star. Frost the top of the tuna with mayonnaise and sprinkle with capers.

• Serve a mélange of mussels, cherrystone clams, chopped tomato, pearl onions, parsley, and white wine baked in a parchment paper envelope and opened at table to release marvelously aromatic vapors.

• Serve a broiled bluefish fillet surrounded by a pond of rich tomato sauce on a large white plate. Lay a sprig of watercress on the fish and place a large lemon wedge over the stems.

• Arrange deep-fried breaded fish fillets in an overlapping row on a large oval platter. Partially insert thin slices of lime between pieces of fish. Lay lemon wedges skin side out around the edge of the platter.

• Serve sautéed scallops on a blue plate. Place a scallop shell filled with pickle-flecked tartar sauce for dipping on the plate with the scallops. Garnish with a decorative lemon half.

• Invert a can of salmon into the cup of a Boston lettuce leaf on a large white plate. Place 1 slice hard-cooked egg on top of the salmon and dot the egg with ½ teaspoon black lumpfish caviar. Garnish with 3 black olives.

Frankfurters

Franks are all-American treats that everyone loves. Here are some colorful ways to dress them:

• SWISS FRANKS   Mustard, sliced franks, and Swiss cheese in a grilled sandwich.

• PIZZA FRANKS   A toasted English muffin, pizza sauce, sliced franks, and shredded mozzarella, broiled until bubbly.

• CHEF'S SALAD   Cut julienne strips from cooked franks and use them in a chef's salad in place of ham or turkey.

• MACARONI AND FRANK SALAD or FRANK AND POTATO SALAD   Cut cooked franks into ½-inch slices, then stir into favorite macaroni or potato salad recipe.

• GLAZED FRANKS   Cut diamond-pattern slashes into grilled franks, drizzle with a little molasses, liquid brown sugar, or dark corn syrup and broil without turning, just until reheated. Serve on a steaming-hot bed of baked beans or in a heated bun with baked beans.

• FRENCH FRANKS   Grilled franks, Dijon mustard, sliced cornichons (small gherkins), and pearl cocktail onions in a 5-inch length of baguette (a long thin loaf of French bread).

• DUTCH FRANKS   Grilled franks, mustard, and hot potato salad served in a warm bun or on a kaiser roll.

• FRANKS ESPAGNOLE   Grilled franks, tomato sauce, sautéed red and green bell peppers, and sliced black olives served on a warm bun.

• PITA FRANKS   Sliced grilled franks, coleslaw, and Thousand Island dressing in a warm pita pocket.

• HOG DOG   Wrap a slice of bacon around each frank, grill or broil until brown, serve on a warm bun.

• DIXIE DOG   Grilled franks, mustard, black-eyed peas served on warm sliced corn bread.

• SOPHISTICATED FRANK   Grilled frank, watercress, sliced raw mushrooms, and crumbled blue cheese served on a 5-inch length of baguette (a long, thin loaf of French bread).

• GARDEN DOG   A warm bun, shredded lettuce, sliced cucumber, a grilled frank, and sliced cherry tomatoes.

• BREAKFAST FRANK   Grilled franks, scrambled eggs, and ketchup served on toast.

• FRANKLY DELIGHTFUL   Grilled franks, mustard, hot sauerkraut, and sliced apples served on a warm bun.

• TEX-MEX DOG   Grilled franks, chili, chopped jalapeño peppers, grated American cheese, served in a tortilla.

Fruit Fillips

• Fill the cavities of canned pear halves with sugar-coated cranberries and place them around a roast turkey. Insert small bunches of watercress in between the pears to set them apart.

• Place a whole strawberry in the cavity of a canned peach half and use to garnish a plate of smoked ham.

• Fill canned apricot halves with blueberries and use to garnish a stack of golden pancakes.

• Place a pineapple ring on a chocolate-brown plate and top it with a scoop of chicken salad sprinkled with blanched almonds. Garnish the plate with a small cluster of seedless green grapes.

- Decorate a large white plate north, east, south, and west, beginning with 4 slices of orange placed in a circle near the center of the plate. Working toward the edge of the plate, top each with an overlapping slice of lemon, and top each lemon slice with an overlapping slice of lime. Place a broiled fillet of bluefish over the decoration so that it shows through underneath. Top the fish with a pat of lemon butter and a light dusting of grated lemon zest.

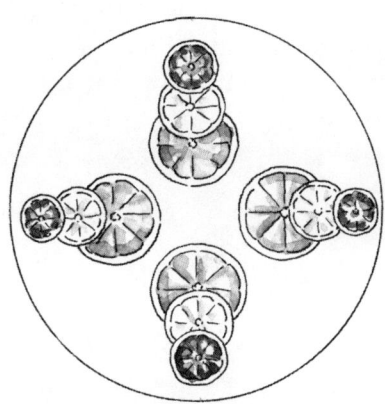

- Hollow out bright red baking apples, leaving a shell about ½ inch thick. Fill with sausage and bread stuffing and bake until cooked through and apples are tender. Place the apples around a roast duck and pile small heaps of sauerkraut between the apples to set them apart.
- Fill the cavity of a halved and seeded papaya with tuna salad. Top the salad with a wedge of hard-cooked egg and place the papaya on a bed of shredded romaine lettuce.
- Slice ripe yellow pears in half lengthwise and remove the core. Spread the cut side of each half with a Roquefort cheese spread and then reassemble the pears so that they once again look whole. Stick a sprig of mint at the top of each pear and serve them on a bed of watercress. •
- Cut a honeydew melon into 6 rings. Peel and scoop out each ring; place on individual crystal salad plates. Arrange diced plums and nectarines and seedless green grapes in centers of melon. Sprinkle with shred-

ded coconut for added flavor and texture, and serve with a honey and lime dressing on the side.

• Halve and pit an avocado and serve a scoop of tomato sherbet in the cavities.

• Slice a cantaloupe in half and remove the seeds. Level off the bottom so that the melon halves stand straight. Chill and serve filled with cherry or plum soup. Garnish with a sprig of mint.

• Fill a hollowed nectarine with lemon sherbet. Cut top off nectarines. Using a small sharp knife, cut around the pit, leaving a ½-inch shell. Fill cavity with a scoop of lemon sherbet and serve in a stemmed crystal wineglass.

Garnishes

Embellishments that can add color and appeal to foods play an important role in food presentation. Roses made from spirals of lemon peel nested in a spray of feathery fresh dill can make a dish of plain poached fish come to life. A few radish roses and a pickle fan can turn a slice of muddy-colored pâté into an elegant, mouth-watering appetizer. There are many things you can use to decorate your food: fruits, vegetables, nuts, hard-cooked eggs, and even flowers. But the most important thing to remember is that any garnish placed directly upon the food should always be edible. Inedible but non-toxic items, such as clamshells, nutshells, and leaves, can be used to decorate trays and platters and centerpieces rather than the food itself.

Remember, too, that garnishes should complement but not overpower any dish. Try to keep them simple so that they draw attention to the food without causing a flamboyant distraction.

Try to avoid garnishes that require a lot of cutting or slicing into soft pulp. For example, use cherry tomatoes instead of cutting large tomatoes into smaller pieces. Any fruit or vegetable that you have to cut into is either going to dry up, turn brown or discolor, or bleed its juices into an unsightly puddle.

Foods, Plain and Fancy   105

Make a point of keeping some fresh parsley, chicory, or escarole on hand in your refrigerator. Curly greenery is very versatile and can quickly be tucked here and there, wherever a colorful garnish is needed at the last moment.

A tip for the busy hostess: garnish your serving plates and platters before your guests arrive. When the food is ready to be served, you save time by simply placing it on the predecorated plates.

If you have a garden, consider covering your trays with masses of green leaves, such as citrus leaves or grape leaves. Other leaves can be picked from trees, flowers, or bushes, perhaps by your children. Even though these aren't meant to be eaten (they're only going to decorate your trays), make sure that you don't pick a poisonous variety, just in case. If you're in doubt, consult a book on toxic plants at the library.

Save such greenery as carrot, celery, beet, radish, and turnip tops. What you might normally consider to be garbage could actually turn out to be a lovely garnish with a little imagination. A few tomato, lemon, or orange roses made from the peelings of the fruit can be placed atop these greens to achieve an attractive bouquet effect.

Many garnishes can be prepared ahead of time and stored in the refrigerator. Your children might love to help you with some of these:

• VEGETABLE CUPS   Make tiny cups from 2-inch lengths of large cooked carrots, or hollow out small turnips or cherry tomatoes. Fill centers with julienne vegetables or a dip mixture.

• CITRUS WEDGES   Save orange, lemon, lime, or grapefruit shells after squeezing juice. Scoop out the moist membrane. The cleaned shells may then be stored and accumulated in your freezer. The day before your party, thaw the shells and make flavored gelatin in contrasting colors. Fill the shells with the liquid gelatin and chill until set. To serve, cut each shell in half to form a wedge.

• PICKLE FANS   Use small whole pickles and cut 4 lengthwise slits from one end to *almost* the other end of each pickle. Gently spread to form an open fan.

• RADISH ROSES   Remove both ends from large radishes. Cut thin petals all around the radishes. Place in a bowl of ice water for at least 1 hour. The petals will open by themselves and the radishes will be cold.

Radish Roses

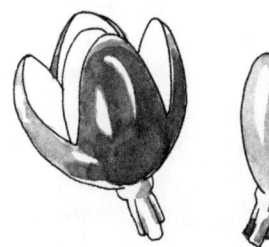

• CELERY CURLS   Cut celery stalks into 4-inch lengths. Slit both ends into narrow strips *almost* to the center. To curl ends and chill, place in a bowl of ice water.

• CARROT CURLS   Peel carrots and cut into paper-thin lengthwise slices with a vegetable peeler or very sharp knife. Roll up and fasten with toothpicks. Chill in ice water. Before serving, remove picks and place a sprig of parsley or an olive in the center of each curl.

• FROSTED FRUITS   Wash and dry small clusters of grapes or use whole cherries or strawberries with stems. Lightly beat one egg white until frothy. Dip the fruit into the egg white; then into extra fine granulated sugar. Dry on racks.

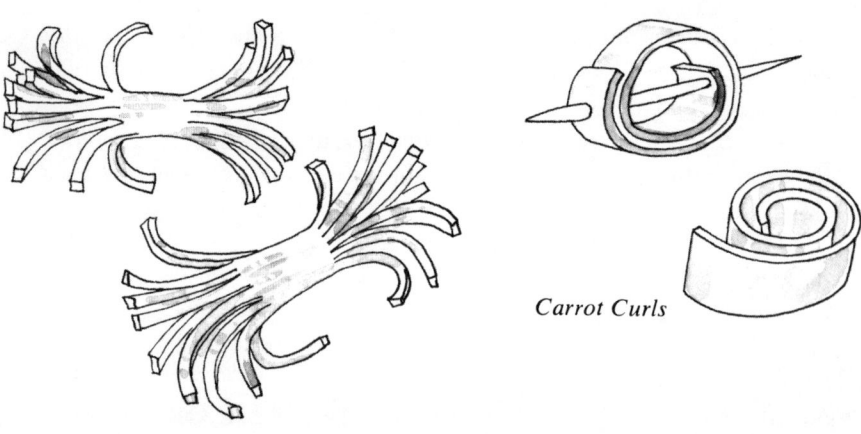

Carrot Curls

Celery Curls

• ONION CHRYSANTHEMUMS   Skin a large onion. Cut off the top but leave the root end intact. From the top to *almost* the bottom, cut thin slits all around the onion. Add several drops of food coloring to a bowl of ice water. Allow the onion to soak several hours to absorb the color and open.

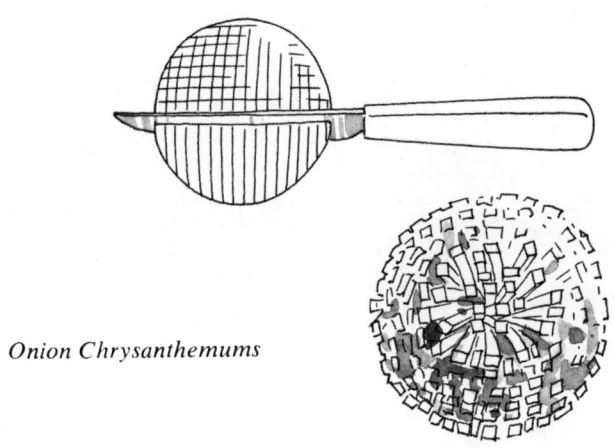

Onion Chrysanthemums

• JULIENNE VEGETABLES   Cut uncooked carrots, celery, zucchini, parsnips, or cooked broccoli stems into narrow matchlike strips. Chill in a bowl of ice water. Arrange in bundles with a strip of pimiento over the top.

• VEGETABLE BASKETS   Halve and hollow out eggplants, bell peppers, zucchini, or yellow squash and fill with your favorite dip or olives, radishes, cherry tomatoes, or small pickles.

• TOMATO ROSES   You can make two kinds of tomato roses. Cut a tomato part way down in sixths or eighths. Then, using a sharp paring knife, peel down the outer skin about a quarter of the way. Or pare the skin off a tomato in one continuous length and coil it to form the rose.

• ORANGE BUTTERFLIES   Using your fingers, peel a naval orange or a tangerine and break the fruit into segments, being careful not to tear the thin membrane. Remove as much of the white pith as possible. Arrange two orange sections, back-to-back, so that they resemble wings. Remove the white pith from underneath the larger pieces of peeled skin. Slice the rind into long, thin strips and place two strips in between each pair of orange wings so that they resemble antennae.

Tomato Rose

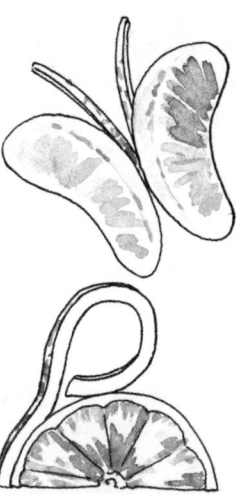

Orange Butterfly

• ORANGE LOOPS Slice an orange in half, lengthwise from stem to stern. Cut each half into ⅜-inch-thick slices. Using a sharp paring knife, cut along the pith of the orange between the skin and the fruit. The cut should start at one end of each slice and go to within 1 inch of the other end, leaving the last inch connected. Curl the loose strip of skin under to form a loop.

• FLOWERS These can be used to garnish foods, adding a romantic or exotic accent. Many are edible, including herb flowers like borage and chives, or garden varieties like black-eyed Susans, calendulas, carnations, red clover, chrysanthemums, columbine (only the roots are edible), daisies, dandelions, daylilies, elderberry flowers, forsythia, geraniums, gladioli, hibiscus, honeysuckle, jasmine, lavender, lemon blossoms, lilacs, marigolds, nasturtiums, orange blossoms, pansies, plum blossoms, roses, tulips, and violets.

• Garnish a grilled chuck steak by laying a few daylilies along the edge of the plate just before serving.

• Garnish a roast leg of lamb with a stalk of gladiolus blossoms placed next to it just before serving.

• Sprinkle a salad with pansy blossoms.

• Sprinkle brown rice with marigold petals.

• Stud a scoop of orange sherbet with single lilac flowers.

• Stuff nasturtiums with ricotta cheese and chopped walnuts. Arrange on top of a tossed green salad.

• Scent and flavor drinking water by combining violets, rose petals, orange blossoms, or forget-me-nots with water in a glass jar. Place in the sun for several hours, chill, strain, and serve with fresh flower blossoms floating in each glass.

• Float lemon blossoms in a sauceboat of melted butter.

❋

Hamburgers

Topped with a zesty, colorful garnish, hamburgers can be nutritious, delicious, and eye-catching. Try some of these combinations to make a burger with a difference:

• HANDY BURGER Hamburger served in a pita pocket with shredded red cabbage, shredded lettuce, bean sprouts, and tahini dressing.

• INTERNATIONAL BURGER Hamburger served on an English muffin and topped with ratatouille.

• REUBEN BURGER Hamburger served on rye bread and topped with Thousand Island dressing, sauerkraut, and grated Swiss cheese.

• TACO BURGER A tortilla spread with mild taco sauce, refried beans, shredded lettuce, a hamburger, and shredded cheddar cheese.

• CALIFORNIA BURGER Hamburger served on sourdough bread, with Russian dressing, shredded lettuce, a slice of tomato, 2 slices of avocado, and a sprinkle of crumbled Gorgonzola.

• HAWAIIAN BURGER Romaine lettuce, a hamburger, a pineapple slice (unsweetened), crumbled blue cheese, and alfalfa sprouts.

• SCRAMBLED BURGER A hamburger, a scrambled egg, sliced cherry tomatoes, and a generous sprinkling of chopped chives.

• BURGER QUEEN A Boston lettuce leaf, a hamburger, sliced tomato, Welsh rabbit, and chopped scallions.

• GREEK BURGER Sliced tomato, sliced black olives, a hamburger, sliced red onion, crumbled feta cheese, and sliced radishes.

• CANADIAN BURGER A hamburger, Canadian bacon, shredded cheddar cheese, and asparagus tips.

• BIG APPLEBURGER A hamburger, shredded lettuce, sliced apple, crumbled blue cheese, and alfalfa sprouts.

• NEW ENGLAND BURGER Boston lettuce, a hamburger, baked beans, shredded Vermont cheddar cheese, and bacon on an English muffin.

• RUSSIAN BURGER A hamburger, sliced hard-cooked egg, sour cream, and red lumpfish caviar.

• ITALIAN BURGER   A hamburger, melted provolone topped with red and green bell pepper rings.

• DELI BURGER   A hamburger on rye, coleslaw, and raisins.

• INDIAN BURGER   A hamburger, sliced cucumber, a dollop of plain yogurt, and a sprinkling of chopped dill.

• PIZZA BURGER   A hamburger, sliced red onion, pizza sauce, and shredded mozzarella.

• SPINACH BURGER   Raw spinach leaves, a hamburger, sliced hard-cooked egg, bacon, and mayonnaise.

• FAVORITE BURGER   A hamburger, a slice of tomato, shredded cheddar cheese—broil until cheese begins to melt.

Ice Ideas

• To intensify the taste and color of cold drinks, freeze ice cubes from appropriate liquids, such as:

Wine Cubes   Serve with iced tea, spritzers, or Kirs.
white— 1 part dry white wine with 3 parts water
red—   1 part dry red wine with 4 parts water
rosé— 1 part rosé wine with 3 parts water

Tea Cubes   Serve with iced tea.
Freeze cooled brewed tea, undiluted.

Coffee Cubes   Serve with iced coffee.
Freeze cooled, undiluted coffee.

Mineral Water Cubes   Serve with mineral water. Note that these may take on a frosty or effervescent appearance.

Fruit Juice Cubes   Great for a party. Freeze orange, pineapple, or tomato juice.

• Cut the peel from oranges, lemons, or limes into long narrow strips; loop and tie into knots. Freeze with water in ice cube trays to garnish cold drinks, such as iced tea, fruit punch, Tom Collinses, apéritifs, diet sodas, or mineral water.

• Dramatize cubes for cocktails by freezing ingredients with water in ice cube trays:

For bloody marys: cherry tomatoes, a lemon rose, or a celery curl.

For martinis: olives, lemon roses, or cocktail onions.

For manhattans, sours, and collinses: maraschino cherries.

For old fashioneds: orange zest roses.

• For a punch, freeze lemonade in a decorative ring mold. When partially frozen, arrange whole strawberries, raspberries, and blueberries around the insides. Freeze until set. Unmold and place in a large bowl to keep punch cold.

• For a buffet, freeze water in a decorative ring mold. When partially frozen, arrange citrus or camellia leaves, daisies, tea rose blossoms, and statice around the insides. Freeze until set. Unmold and place decorated ice ring on a large platter. Fill the center with radish roses and celery curls, and surround the ring with seedless green grapes.

Meat and Poultry

• Cut bologna *with skin* into ⅛-inch-thick slices. Spread one side with butter and place the slices buttered side up on a baking sheet. Place 3 inches from fire under a preheated broiler. As the slices heat up, they will take the shape of cups. Remove from broiler and fill with hot peas. Arrange on a platter with tomato wedges as a garnish.

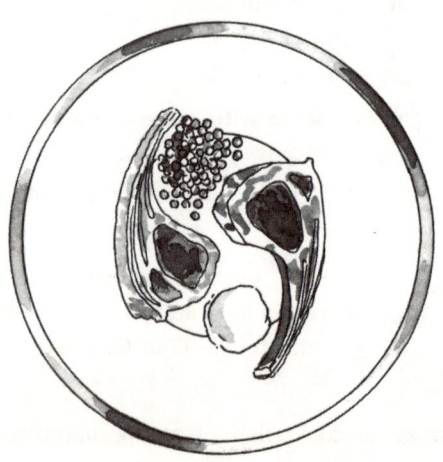

- Arrange 2 cooked rib pork chops in opposite directions on a dinner plate so that the rib bones form the shape of an S. Place a scoop of mashed turnips next to the curve of one chop and a mound of peas next to the curve of the other chop.

- Serve creamed chicken in the cavity of a halved avocado nestled in buttered egg noodles.

- Serve beef curry in the cavity of a halved cantaloupe with the bottom leveled off so that it stands steady and straight.

- Thinly slice 2 boiled new potatoes and spread them in an overlapping row down the center of a yellow plate. Place a grilled shoulder lamb chop on one side of the potato line and arrange 8 steamed snow peas in a row to form 4 sets of "xxxx" on the other side of the potato line.

- Unmold a meat loaf baked in a bowl onto a large round plate and surround it with mounds of mashed rutabaga separated with small bundles of steamed whole green beans.

Oils

- Enhance the flavor, aroma, and texture of foods by giving them a change of oil. Light and delicate, such as safflower or sunflower, fruity, such as olive oil, or unctuous and pungent, such as sesame or walnut, the variety of oil you select can create a whole new experience for the mouth. Try peanut oil for browning meat, olive oil for lightly frying fish, walnut or sesame oil for salad dressings. Here are some other suggestions:

- Arrange a plate of sliced vine-ripened tomatoes with overlapping, alternating slices of mozzarella cheese. Dress only with tatters of fresh basil and a liberal sprinkling of cold-pressed extra virgin olive oil.

- Brush fruity virgin olive oil over thick slices of fresh Italian bread. Rub with split, peeled garlic cloves and toast under the broiler until golden.

- Combine fragrant walnut oil with sherry vinegar and use to dress artichoke hearts, warm potato salad, a cold brown rice salad, or a warm combination of steamed green beans, thinly sliced calf's liver, and cubed avocado.

Pastry Dough

• Roll out dough and use aspic or cookie cutters to make attractive shapes, such as hearts, stars, or diamonds, that can be arranged on top of a pâté en croûte, a berry pie, or a steak and kidney pudding.

• For a golden-brown crust, brush the top pastry with milk before baking.

• When making a lattice-topped pie, twist the strips of pastry dough for a pretty effect.

• Mix ¼ cup finely chopped walnuts or pecans into sweet pie pastry dough for a crunchy textured crust.

• Stir 1 teaspoon grated lemon zest into the pastry dough for a chicken potpie for added interest.

• Stir 2 tablespoons fresh snipped dill into the pastry dough for a mushroom quiche for added aroma and flavor.

• When cutting biscuits, cut half the dough with a round biscuit cutter, the other half with a doughnut cutter of the same proportions. Place the doughnut-cut shape on top of the round shape and bake according to your directions. Fill the biscuit containers with creamed chicken and insert 3 asparagus tips into the center of each.

Pie Crimping

A decorative border can transform any pie into a glamorous creation. To make a professional-looking, even crimp, line a pie plate with rolled out pastry dough. Trim the edge of the dough, leaving a ½-inch overhang. Fold the overhang under so that the folded edge is even with the rim of the pie plate. Flatten the edge slightly by gently pressing down with your fingers. This folded, double layer of pastry will not only strengthen the edge of your pie, but will also give you more dough to work with. The doubled dough border can now be crimped into one of the several patterns shown below, or into an original design of your own.

1. Pinch: Position left index finger inside of pastry rim, right index finger and thumb on outside. Pinch outside fingers together shaping the dough into a wavy pattern.

G. TORGENSEN/WOMAN'S DAY STUDIO

Palm-frond fans make practical as well as pretty place mats.

WOMAN'S DAY STUDIO

Color is perhaps the most exciting ingredient that one can use for visual impact when presenting food. A single portion of sherbet takes on new interest when it is served in a wineglass and garnished with a verdant sprig of mint. A grape leaf placed between the glass and the serving dish adds the final touch.

VICTOR SCOOZA
A variety of sandwich ideas results from combining flavors, colors, and textures with your imagination.

A canned ham can be lifted out of the ordinary by serving it with pineapple slices and a garnish of pear halves stuffed with sugar-coated cranberries.
BILL HELMS

Add charm to a meal by serving it in individual baskets that can be carried to your porch, patio, or family room.

Foods, Plain and Fancy 115

2. Flounce: Place right index finger and thumb about 1½ inches apart on pastry rim. Use left index finger to pull out pastry between fingers, shaping the dough into a graceful ruffle.

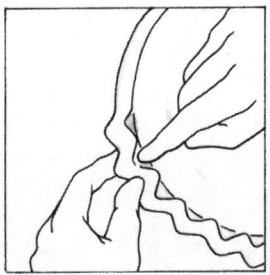 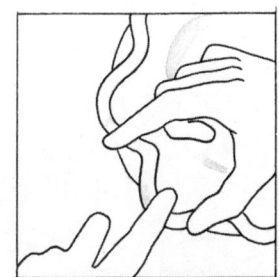

3. Spoon: Using the tip of an inverted teaspoon, press down onto the pastry edge, cutting the dough into a scalloped pattern. For larger scallops, use the tip of an inverted tablespoon.

4. Knife: Grasp a dull-edged dinner knife in the right hand. Press the handle into the dough at regular ½-inch intervals to form an attractive grooved pattern.

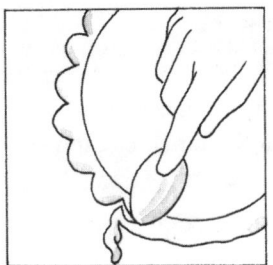 

5. Cutouts: Press pastry trimmings into a ball, flatten slightly and roll out. Use small aspic or garnishing cutters to cut out the rolled dough. Choose a simple design that will look attractive when it is overlapped; such as small circles, stars, diamonds, daisy or leaf shapes. Moisten the

rim of the pie and place the moistened cutouts, slightly overlapping, around the rim. Press into place.

6. Fork: Using the tines of a fork, press firmly around the edge of the pie at ¾-inch intervals. If the dough is sticky, dip the tines in flour from time to time.

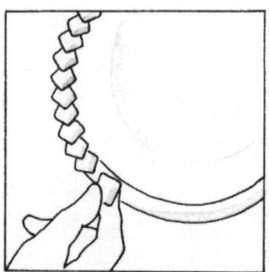 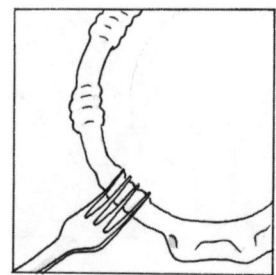

Potatoes

• Use a pastry bag to pipe a small decorative mound of mashed potatoes, or to make a thin border around meat, vegetables, or the plate itself.

• Serve mashed potatoes with an ice cream scoop.

• Serve mashed sweet potatoes or yams in hollowed-out apples. Scoop out inside of baking apples, leaving a margin of about ¼ inch all around. Stuff with golden potatoes and bake in a buttered ovenproof dish at 325° F. until apples are tender, about 20 minutes.

• Fill decorative, hollowed-out orange halves with mashed sweet potatoes. Top with a layer of mini-marshmallows. Bake at 400° F. for about 15 minutes, until marshmallows are browned.

• Place a layer of golden pineapple rings on a buttered baking sheet. Use a pastry bag to pipe mashed sweet potatoes on top of the pineapple rings. Bake at 400° F. until heated through, about 10 minutes.

• Layer pan-browned sausage patties in a buttered pie dish. Use a pastry bag to pipe white or sweet potatoes on top of the patties. Baste with a few teaspoons of sausage drippings for added flavor. Bake at 350° F. for 15 minutes, until heated through.

• Bake potatoes in their jackets and cut the cooked spuds in half lengthwise. Scoop out the potato. Use the hollowed potato shells as edible containers for creamed spinach or other vegetables. Or mash the potato with butter and milk and return it to the skin. Sprinkle with grated cheese.

• Omit the foil and rub baking potatoes with vegetable oil before popping them into a preheated oven. The skin will come out especially crisp and tasty.

• For an elegant treat that is also colorful and appealing, cut a cross in the top of baked potatoes and push the ends of each potato together until the crevice opens. Top with a generous dollop of sour cream, then cap with a spoonful of red lumpfish caviar. Or, if you prefer, serve sour cream, red caviar, and snipped fresh chives on the side. The toppings can be placed in crystal punch cups set on a large crystal plate.

Rice

• For more intense flavor, replace the water in your rice recipe with an equal amount of chicken or beef stock.

• To make pink rice, replace half the liquid required in your rice recipe with an equal quantity of tomato juice.

• For a delicious difference, dress up plain rice: In the pan that you normally use to cook your rice, sauté a chopped onion in 2 or 3 tablespoons of melted butter. When the onion is limp and transparent, stir in 1 cup raw rice. Add the liquid as directed, cover, and bring to a boil. Lower heat and simmer until the liquid is absorbed and the rice is dry.

• Add a spice of your choice to the basic sautéed onion routine described above. *Just a pinch* of nutmeg, coriander, cumin, ground ginger, or cinnamon, for example, can be stirred into the sautéed onion before adding the rice and cooking it.

• Chopped vegetables make tasty additions to rice. Sauté a chopped onion in 2 or 3 tablespoons of butter until limp. Stir in one or more of the following and cook slightly before adding the rice and liquid: a finely minced garlic clove, 1 or 2 tablespoons of minced shallot, 1 stalk of finely chopped celery or fennel, or a diced tomato.

• Many herbs can add interest to plain rice. Simply chop a fresh herb, such as parsley, dill, basil, or chives, and stir 1 tablespoon (or more) into the cooked rice together with 1 tablespoon of butter.

• A diced or grated carrot or a finely chopped small red or green bell pepper can be stirred into your rice about 7 minutes before it is finished cooking. This will add color as well as flavor and texture sensations.

• Stir freshly grated cheese, such as Gruyère, Parmesan, or Romano, into the hot rice before serving for an appetizing variation.

• Cold rice combined with a cup of chopped cooked meat and/or vegetables makes a delightfully delicious and colorful salad when molded. Pack cooked rice into a lightly oiled decorative mold or loaf pan. Chill for several hours. Unmold before serving. For vegetarians, add a jar of marinated artichoke hearts along with the oil in which they're packed and a handful of chopped cashews.

• Leftover rice can add nutrition as well as interest when stirred into soup, stew, an omelet, a salad, a cup of hot milk, or a meat or fruit stuffing mixture.

• Use an ice cream scoop to serve perfect mounds of rice. Arrange the mounds on a platter and separate them with small bundles of green beans placed between the mounds.

Salads

Salads have become staples in the American diet whether they are served as appetizer, main course, or before dessert. Their wide appeal is based upon the belief that they can be low in calories and high in nutrition, but most of all they appeal because they can look so colorful and attractive. One can hardly go wrong chopping up a bunch of fresh vegetables and fruit and combining them in a bowl. To go a step beyond the ordinary, however, does require some imagination and we offer some suggestions here:

- Search out attractive containers for your salads. For instance:

    Large basket can be lined with the outside leaves from red cabbage, savoy cabbage, green cabbage, or romaine lettuce leaves. Line the basket with clear plastic before laying in the leaves so that it is completely waterproofed.

    Soup tureen that has a wide opening is ideal.

    An enameled or copper colander can be lined with clear plastic and the outside leaves from cabbage or lettuce.

    A serving tray can be lined with a plastic table mat and fruits or vegetables arranged in colorful rows, side by side.

    An ice bucket, if it's attractive, can be used as is and will help keep the salad cold as well as provide a container. Other ice buckets can be dressed with a piece of pretty fabric tied around with a matching ribbon.

    New plastic flower pots can make an unusual presentation.

    Glass mixing bowls in bright primary colors like red, blue, or sunshine yellow.

    A 5-quart enamel-over-cast-iron Dutch oven in orange, chocolate brown, or avocado green.

    A crystal punch bowl or a milk glass fruit bowl.

- For a colorful salad, leave raw cucumbers, zucchini, and yellow summer squash unpeeled to add color and texture as well as additional nutrients. Just before using, scrub with a soft brush under running cold water. Or, for a striped effect, peel off intermittently spaced strips of skin. Slice on the bias (at a slanted angle) to vary the cut from the usual rounds.

- A slice of Boursault cheese served on a ruffled leaf of romaine lettuce and garnished with overlapping radish slices is an excellent solution to serving a salad and cheese course at the same time. This is an especially useful combination at a large party when dishes are at a premium. Try it with any salad leaf and a slice of your favorite semi-soft cheese, such as Brie, Explorateur, or Corolle.

- Skewered salads make a delightful presentation. You'll need a heavy, steady base in which to stick the skewers, such as a half head of cabbage, a small pumpkin, half a melon, a pineapple, a large eggplant, or a marrow squash. The base can be placed in a large bowl or on a tray (cut side down). Shape a small aluminum foil wreath to be placed around the bottom of your base if it needs steadying. Surround the base with a mixture of chopped, torn, or shredded salad such as lettuce or cabbage, grated carrots, or Belgian endives. Thread 6-, 8-, or 10-inch skewers with alternating chunks of fruit, vegetables, cheese, and cold cuts, such as:

Fruit
pineapple chunks
melon balls or cubes
papaya cubes
seedless grapes
pitted Bing cherries
apple chunks
pear chunks
orange segments
whole strawberries
cherry tomatoes

Vegetables
bell pepper chunks, red or green
pitted olives, green or black
button mushrooms
small onions
zucchini slices
yellow summer squash slices
steamed broccoli flowerets
steamed cauliflower flowerets
artichoke hearts, marinated
radishes, trimmed

Cheese Cubes
Havarti
Swiss
Gouda
American
mozzarella
Gruyère
provolone
Brie (chilled and underripe
   for firmness)

Cold Cuts/Meat/Fish (cooked)
shrimp, peeled
meatballs, browned
Italian sausage chunks
frankfurter chunks
ham, cubes or folded
salami, cubes or folded
bologna, cubes or folded
chicken, chunks
roast beef, sliced and folded

Firmly stick the threaded skewers into the fruit or vegetable base. To serve, have each person take some mixed salad and a skewer. Salad dressings should be available on the side.

• Present a layered salad in a transparent glass soufflé dish. With the exception of leafy greens, toss each vegetable separately in dressing before placing in the bowl. Select colorful salad ingredients and layer them like a rainbow. Here are six salad suggestions:

Layers from Top of Dish to Bottom

bacon bits	red onion rings	sliced scallions
sliced green beans	orange segments	pineapple chunks
sliced cherry tomatoes	quartered radishes	ham cubes
cubes of Havarti cheese	sliced mushrooms	Swiss cheese chunks
torn Boston lettuce	raw spinach	torn romaine lettuce

croutons and parsley	shredded coconut	pomegranate seeds
halved cherry tomatoes	cubed nectarines	orange segments
Gouda cheese chunks	purple grapes (seeded)	seedless green grapes
shredded iceberg lettuce	watermelon chunks	diced purple plums
cooked white navy beans	halved Bing cherries	sliced peaches

• Off-dry (sem-sweet) white wines can be poured over the layered fruit salads instead of salad dressing. Appropriate selections would include: American Chablis or Sauternes, Chenin Blanc, Johannisberg Riesling, or Extra-dry Champagne or sparkling wine.

• Dip whole strawberries into sour cream, then into strawberry-flavored gelatin granules for an eye-catching flavorful coating. Serve in the hollow of a lettuce leaf on a glass plate.

• Slice red, green, and yellow bell peppers into thin, round circles. Arrange overlapping rings of alternating colors over leaves of Belgian endive. Drizzle with walnut oil and a little fresh lemon juice, and season to taste with salt, freshly ground black pepper, and chopped walnuts.

Salad Toppings

Edible garnishes can make salads special by adding flavor, texture, and visual appeal. Try accessorizing your salads with some of these suggestions:

• NUTS, UNSALTED Chopped pecans or walnuts, sliced blanched almonds, toasted pine nuts (pignoli), or halved cashews or pistachios.

• SEEDS   Hulled, toasted sesame seeds or sunflower seeds, caraway seeds or poppy seeds.

• BREAKFAST CEREALS   Crushed corn or wheat flakes, Grape-Nuts, granola, or wheat germ.

• CROUTONS OR TOASTED BREAD CUBES   Cut leftover bread (white, whole wheat, or rye) into ½-inch cubes. Sauté them in butter or bacon fat until golden. Drain on paper towels and cool before serving.

• FRESH HERBS   Snipped, minced, or chopped chives, parsley, basil, dill weed, mint, tarragon, or chervil.

• VEGETABLE TRIMMINGS   Chopped fennel leaves, celery leaves, carrot tops, or beet tops.

• SPROUTS   Alfalfa and bean or lentil sprouts.

• FRESH FRUIT   Pomegranate seeds, pitted Bing cherries, blueberries or sliced strawberries, seedless grapes, diced purple plums, peaches or nectarines, diced pineapple, or shreds of orange or lemon rind, sliced kiwi, quartered figs.

• CANNED FRUIT   Mandarin orange segments, diced pineapple.

• DRIED FRUIT   Golden or seedless raisins, chopped dates or figs, shredded coconut.

• FRESH VEGETABLES   Sliced mushrooms, radishes, chopped scallions, shredded carrots or parsnips, grated raw beets, rings of red, green, or yellow bell peppers, red or white onion rings, chopped celery or fennel stalks, sliced cucumber, zucchini or yellow squash.

• CANNED VEGETABLES   Diced or sliced beets, garbanzo beans, kidney beans, sliced green beans, corn kernels, asparagus tips, sliced hearts of palm, artichoke hearts, diced carrots. (Drain well.)

• PICKLES AND GARNITURES   Capers, baby corncobs, black or green olives, pimiento strips, gherkins.

• MEATS   Shreds of prosciutto ham, bacon bits, or julienne slices of salami, ham, roast beef, roast pork, roast lamb, or diced chicken or duck.

• FISH   Flaked smoked fish such as salmon or whitefish; flaked canned fish such as tuna or salmon; flaked fresh poached fish such as cod, flounder, weakfish; canned or fresh shellfish such as crab meat or lobster meat; canned smoked fish such as oysters; or boneless sardines or anchovies.

• EGGS   A whole poached egg (well drained); or hard-cooked egg, sliced, chopped, or cut into thin wedges; sieved hard-cooked egg white or yolk.

• CHEESE   Shredded cheddar, Gruyère, or mozzarella; julienne slices of Swiss, muenster, or American; crumbled blue, Roquefort, or feta; grated Parmesan or Romano; diced Brie or Gouda.

Sandwiches

Sandwich making is almost an art form, requiring a delicacy of touch, a symmetrical eye, and an appreciation of proportions. Skillfully done, there are compensations in the very satisfactory results from the many possible combinations of ingredients involving flavors, colors, and textures.

All kinds of bread, wafers, sweetened and unsweetened crackers are used for sandwiches; and every sort of fruit, vegetable, fish, fowl, and meat enters into their composition. Beyond the usual two slices of bread stuffed with anything, suggestions follow for creating and presenting colorful, amusing, and attractive sandwiches.

• TOASTED CHEESE ROLL-UPS   Here's an inviting twist on the grilled cheese sandwich, and one which small children will find easy to hold.

Roll white or whole wheat slices of bread with a rolling pin to make them more flexible. Spread each slice with a small amount of softened butter and mustard and top with a slice of your favorite cheese, such as Swiss, muenster, mozzarella, or American, or shredded Gruyère, Gouda, or Jarlsberg. Place a thin asparagus stalk or a whole green bean (raw or steamed) at one end of the cheese slice and trim the vegetable to fit. Beginning at the vegetable end, roll up each sandwich like a jelly roll and secure with a toothpick. Place under a broiler and toast lightly on all sides, turning frequently. Remove toothpicks and serve hot from a bread basket lined with a green and white striped napkin with 3 or 4 lemon leaves tucked here and there.

• ROLLED SANDWICHES   Cut the crusts from thin slices of soft bread, white or whole wheat, and roll them with a rolling pin to make them more flexible. Spread with softened butter and your choice of filling (see some suggestions below) and sprinkle with a small amount of shredded lettuce, alfalfa sprouts, watercress leaves, or raw spinach for added color. Place a ¼-inch-thick slice of red or green bell pepper at one end and roll up the sandwich like a jelly roll. Wrap each roll tightly in plastic wrap and refrigerate until well chilled. Place 2 or 3 wrapped sandwiches in a lunch box with an apple or pear and a couple of oatmeal cookies. Or take them on a picnic: wrap packages of a similar size with carrot and celery sticks and stand these upright with the wrapped sandwiches in a painted tin box lined with a blue bandana.

Filling Suggestions: Combine all ingredients and spread on bread. Portions may be increased as desired.

Chicken Liver and Bacon (2 servings)

½ cup mashed cooked chicken livers
3 slices bacon, cooked and crumbled
1 tablespoon softened butter
1 tablespoon minced parsley
1 tablespoon finely chopped raisins
1 tablespoon dry sherry (optional)

Chicken (2 servings)

½ cup finely minced or ground cooked chicken
¼ cup minced celery
1 tablespoon finely chopped black olives
2 tablespoons mayonnaise

Chicken and Pineapple (2 servings)

½ cup finely minced or ground cooked chicken
2 tablespoons finely minced celery
2 tablespoons crushed pineapple, drained
2 tablespoons mayonnaise

Egg and Avocado (2 servings)

1 hard-cooked egg, finely chopped or sieved
½ cup mashed avocado

2 teaspoons lemon juice
1 tablespoon mayonnaise
1 tablespoon chopped sweet pickle

Tuna or Salmon with Cucumber (2 servings)

½ cup flaked, cooked or canned tuna or salmon
¼ cup mayonnaise
2 tablespoons chopped cucumber
1 tablespoon small capers
1 teaspoon minced parsley

Tongue (2 servings)

½ cup finely minced or ground cooked tongue
2 tablespoons finely minced celery
1 tablespoon small capers
2 black olives, finely minced
2 tablespoons mayonnaise

Egg Salad (2 servings)

2 hard-cooked eggs, finely chopped or sieved
2 tablespoons mayonnaise
2 teaspoons ketchup
2 tablespoons chopped sweet pickle

Peanut Butter and Banana (2 servings)

½ cup peanut butter
2 tablespoons mayonnaise
½ banana, peeled and mashed

Meat (1 serving)

¼ cup ground, cooked meat (roast beef, steak, lamb, veal, or pork)
1 tablespoon mayonnaise
1 teaspoon chopped parsley

• WAFFLE SANDWICHES Spread white or whole wheat bread slices with your choice of filling (see our suggestion below), close sandwich, lightly spread the outside with a small amount of butter. Toast in a hot waffle iron until browned. Serve warm on a red plate with a cluster of seedless green grapes.

For 2 sandwiches: Mix ⅓ cup softened cream cheese, 3 tablespoons drained crushed pineapple, and 1 tablespoon chopped fresh chives. Spread on inside of 4 bread slices, crusts removed. Close each sandwich, placing a slice of boiled ham in the center of each.

• PINWHEEL SANDWICHES You will need 1 loaf of unsliced white or whole wheat bread, softened butter and sandwich fillings. For suggestions see previous page.

Cut the side, end, and bottom crusts from an unsliced loaf of bread. Do not remove the top crust yet, as it is easier to grasp the loaf at this end. Cut a thin (about ¼ inch) and as even a slice as possible from the bottom of the loaf—the long way. Cut the remaining loaf into similar pieces. Roll each slice with a rolling pin to make it more flexible. Spread one side of each slice with softened butter and your choice of sandwich filling. Starting at one end of the slice (a short end), roll up tightly like a jelly roll. Wrap in a damp cloth and refrigerate for at least 1 hour. Prepare all of the slices in this manner.

To serve, cut each roll crosswise into pinwheels about ¼ to ½ inch thick. Arrange overlapping slices on a platter or tray lined with a pink linen towel. Edge the tray with tea rose blossoms and small bunches of parsley.

• CHECKERBOARD FINGER SANDWICHES One of the most spectacular ways of presenting finger sandwiches is by arranging them in the pattern of a chess or checkerboard. The results are so outstanding that it's hard to believe such a witty presentation can ever be put together by a child.

Just as red and black are the classic color combinations of a checkerboard, so too are caviar and smoked salmon classic canapé combinations.

You will need 7 slices of white or whole wheat bread to make a checkerboard that is 5 squares × 5 squares (3 squares will be left over). Or you will need 21 slices of bread to make a checkerboard 9 squares × 9 squares (3 squares left over). Remove the crusts from each slice of bread.

Spread softened whipped cream cheese on 4 (or on 11 for the larger amount) slices of thinly sliced bread. Sprinkle with freshly grated black pepper and completely cover each slice with thinly sliced smoked salmon. Cut each slice into 4 squares.

Spread softened whipped butter on 3 (or 10) slices of bread. Spread completely with black lumpfish caviar. Cut each slice into 4 squares.

To assemble, begin and end with a square of salmon, arranging the salmon and caviar squares alternately in a checkerboard pattern on a large plate or cardboard backing cut to fit. Tuck parsley sprigs around the edge of the board.

Other checkerboard combinations:

• red lumpfish caviar and black lumpfish caviar on cream cheese

• thinly sliced boiled ham and sliced American cheese on bread spread with butter and mustard

• chopped, pitted black olives on cream cheese and grated carrots on cream cheese

• sieved hard-cooked egg yolk and sieved hard-cooked egg white on buttered bread

• CLUB SANDWICHES A three-decker sandwich (made with 3 slices of bread) may be perfect for someone with a hearty appetite, but it is also just the right size for sharing with a child, a friend, or a partner for a snack or a light lunch. The trick of presenting these large sandwiches with eye appeal lies in the final cut. This is how it's done:

1. Toast 3 slices of white, whole wheat, or rye bread.

2. Spread one side of each with butter, mayonnaise, Thousand Island dressing, or tartar sauce.

3. Top one slice with turkey and bacon, ham and cheese, chicken salad, tuna salad, or egg salad. Cover with the second slice. Top with lettuce and tomato, watercress, and thinly sliced onion, or raw spinach and crumbled blue cheese. Top with the third slice, dressing side down. Press slightly.

4. *Imagine* that you are going to slice the sandwich into an X (4 triangles) and, with this in mind, place a frilled party pick (toothpick) in the center of each triangle to secure the layers. This will prevent the sandwich from falling apart so that you can now cut it into 4 triangles.

5. Place the triangles with the toothpicks holding them together, crust side down, on a large oval plate and garnish with pickle spears.

• MINIATURE SANDWICHES. These can be served with tea, a coffee break, an afternoon or midnight snack. Colorful, dainty finger sandwiches are irresistibly charming, and they can be assembled quickly. Serve on doily-covered plates or on a tray lined with grape leaves.

• Remove crusts and spread thinly sliced white bread with creamed butter and chopped mint leaves. Cut into 4 triangles and place a thin cucumber slice on each. Top with ¼ teaspoon of red lumpfish caviar.

• Remove crusts and spread thinly sliced white bread with butter or margarine. Cut into 4 squares and cover each square with colorful petals of nasturtium flowers. Top with a thin slice of hard-cooked egg, allowing some of the petals to peep through underneath. Lightly dust the yolk with paprika.

• Toast English muffins, butter, and cut into quarters. Spread each quarter with softened cream cheese and spoon a smidgen of orange marmalade in the center.

• Butter thin rounds of Swedish pumpernickel and spread with a thin layer of tuna fish. Arrange semicircles of thinly sliced celery around the edge.

• Spread thin slices of whole wheat bread with equal parts of butter and mashed sardines. Cut into triangles and top with a thin slice of cherry tomato.

- Mash half a ripe avocado, add 2 tablespoons of lime juice, salt, freshly ground black pepper, a dash of hot pepper sauce, and 1 tablespoon of chopped pimiento. Mound onto toast squares and top with sliced, pitted black olives.

- OPEN-FACE SANDWICHES In Denmark the open-face sandwich is a lunchbox favorite for everyone in the family. Meats, fish, cheeses, fruits, and vegetables artfully arranged on a slice of firm bread can be substantial enough to serve as a snack for 2 (or 1), or a light meal that'll be a lunch break hit. Or you can create an open-face sandwich buffet.

Choose the toppings that appeal to you: thinly sliced cold cuts, such as salami, ham, liverwurst, or bologna; leftovers from a roast or steak; marinated herring or boneless sardines; and slices of cheese such as Swiss, Muenster, or Jarlsberg. Folding the slices and overlapping them makes room for more. A colorful garnish adds the finishing touch: hard-cooked egg, radish, or raw mushroom slices; watercress or parsley sprigs; sprouts; tomato wedges, onion rings; cucumber twists; carrot or celery curls, to name a few. Whatever you include, remember that an open-face sandwich must always be attractive. The visual appeal, rather than complexity of ingredients, is what makes it special.

You can select a few of the open-face sandwich themes that follow or devise your own colorful and delicious combinations:

- Generously cover a slice of whole wheat toast with peanut butter. Leaving a ¾-inch peanut butter border, spread 2 tablespoons of ricotta cheese on top and lightly sprinkle with cinnamon. Swirl a spoonful of honey over the cheese and press 4 red apple slices in a row into the cheese, skin side up. Serve on a red plastic plate.

- Spread slices of French bread with ripe Brie. Fold a slice of boiled ham around 2 canned asparagus spears and insert the ham roll through the center of a pineapple ring. Place on the prepared bread and tuck a few sprigs of watercress around the pineapple for garnish.

- Spread white toast with butter. Top with 3 overlapping slices of tomato. Sprinkle with fresh chopped parsley and arrange 2 boneless sardines on top. Garnish with thinly sliced red onion rings.

- Spread toasted rye bread with guacamole (avocado dip). Leaving a ½-inch border, cover the sandwich with slices of hard-cooked egg topped with tiny shrimp. Place each sandwich on a small black-lacquered tray and garnish with a wedge of lime and a lemon twist.

• Spread pumpernickel bread with butter and cover with shredded iceberg lettuce. Top with marinated herring covered with thinly sliced red onion rings. Garnish with sprigs of fresh dill. Serve on a blue plate with one pickled beet.

• Spread pumpernickel bread with liverwurst. Sprinkle with crumbled bacon. Place a thinly sliced red onion ring in the center and arrange a row of sliced raw mushrooms on top. Serve on a green plate with a cherry tomato for garnish.

• Spread pumpernickel bread with butter and crumbled blue cheese. Leaving a border, sprinkle center area with alfalfa sprouts. Arrange sliced cherry tomatoes in a diagonal overlapping row from one corner of the bread to the other. Serve on a large white plate next to a trimmed scallion and 2 black olives.

• Spread sliced Italian bread with olive oil and grated mozzarella cheese. Arrange an overlapping row of cooked sweet or hot Italian sausage, sliced on the bias, along the center of the bread. Top with one red, one yellow, and one green bell pepper ring.

• Spread toasted rye bread with butter and cover with 2 overlapping slices of Swiss cheese, trimmed to fit. Cut 2 slices of salami into quarters and arrange the triangles overlapping down the center of the cheese. Fan a sliced green olive and place it at the base of the top salami triangle.

• Spread a slice of white bread with butter and completely cover with raw spinach leaves. Arrange 4 slices of hard-cooked egg in the center. Press canned tuna fish into tiny decorative tartlet molds and unmold one per sandwich in the center of the eggs. Top with a pinch of red lumpfish caviar.

• Spread pumpernickel bread with butter and top with curly chicory leaves. Arrange overlapping folded slices of rare roast beef on top of the chicory and top with a fried egg sprinkled with grated Gruyère cheese.

• Butter cracked wheat bread and line with raw spinach. Place a small scoop of chicken salad in the center and top with a marinated artichoke heart. Serve on an orange plate garnished with a trimmed scallion.

• Spread sliced oatmeal bread with Russian dressing. Fold slices of turkey and Monterey Jack cheese in half and alternately arrange them in an overlapping pattern on the bread. Garnish with a small heap of coleslaw sprinkled with seedless raisins.

• TREASURE CHEST OF SANDWICHES   You will need: 1 loaf of unsliced white or whole wheat bread, softened butter, sandwich fillings (see suggestions earlier in this chapter), and parsley for garnish:

Slice off the rounded top (about a fourth to a third of the bread) from a loaf of uncut bread and set it aside. To hollow the loaf, turn it upside down to rest on the cut end. Use a sharp pointed knife (a serrated steak knife is good) and cut through the bottom of the loaf (all the way through), leaving a ½-inch margin around the edge. Push the inside of the loaf out in one piece. Slice off the bottom crust and replace it in the loaf shell.

Cut the bread from the center into slices and make sandwiches, using one or more fillings.

Place the loaf shell on a stainless steel tray lined with a red linen hand towel. Line the inside of the loaf with aluminum foil. Arrange or stack the sandwiches inside. Garnish the edges with fresh parsley and cover the chest with the top of the loaf.

• FROSTED SANDWICH CAKE   You will need: a round loaf of rye bread or a rectangular loaf of white or whole wheat bread, unsliced, softened butter, 6 to 8 servings each of 2 different sandwich fillings (see suggestions earlier in this chapter), 8 ounces softened cream cheese, 1 tablespoon milk, ½ cup yellow cheese spread. For garnish, sliced cucumbers and parsley.

Trim off all crust from bread and level by slicing off the top third. Reserve the top for another use. Slice bread lengthwise into 3 layers. Spread one layer with one of your filling choices, top with another layer spread with the other filling, and top with the third slice. Transfer to a crystal cake plate.

Whip cream cheese with milk until fluffy; frost the top and sides of the sandwich cake, reserving ¼ cup cream cheese. Combine reserved cream cheese with the yellow cheese spread and, using a pastry tube, pipe a decorative border at the base of the cake and around the top edge. Tuck parsley around the base and press sliced cucumbers around the sides and in an overlapping pattern on top of the cake. Serves 6 to 8.

✳

Soups

• Serve pumpkin bisque in a scooped-out pumpkin.

• Scrape out all the flesh from your morning cantaloupe or grapefruit half, leaving a clean shell. Freeze until very cold. Fill with jellied consommé and top with a mint sprig.

• Chill large balloon-shaped wineglasses and fill with cold borsch or cold cucumber soup. Float a dollop of sour cream on top and sprinkle with chopped chives. Serve the glass with a pretty floral-patterned saucer underneath.

• Serve tomato bisque in demitasse cups and garnish with the top leafy part of a celery stalk.

• Serve a cold, spicy mulligatawny soup in a halved coconut shell steadied in a bowl of crushed ice.

• Serve cold bouillon in a tall frosted glass with a straw for sipping. Insert a daisy into the straw. (Remove flower before sipping!)

• Serve a chilled peach or cherry soup in a shallow crystal bowl. Garnish with 5 seedless green grapes, 6 blueberries, and a sprig of mint.

• Serve watercress soup in a hollowed-out green bell pepper with a sprig of watercress for garnish. Choose a steady pepper.

• Pour cream of carrot soup into blue bowls from a blue earthenware pitcher. Garnish with an orange-peel rose.

• Just before serving, add a jewellike garnish of finely diced red bell peppers to split pea soup.

• Float a colorful garnish of 3 thinly sliced radishes on red bowl filled with lentil soup.

Tea

• Use honey, maple syrup, or undiluted fruit juice concentrates as flavorful sweeteners for a change of pace.

• Serve tea from your favorite coffeepot, just because it's something different and unexpected. If a coffee aroma has permeated the container, soak it with a solution of baking soda and water for several hours. Rinse well.

• For a flavor bonus, pour a tablespoon of dark rum, brandy, or your favorite liqueur into each cup. A splash of vodka in a cup of peppermint tea, for example, is a delightful treat that warms the heart.

• Place a cinnamon stick in each cup of hot tea. This will heighten both the aroma and the flavor.

• Serve tea, iced or hot, with an orange slice hooked over the edge of the cup or glass. Or serve with a wedge of lime in place of the usual lemon.

• Keep brewed tea at room temperature to prevent clouding. If clouding occurs, you can clear the tea by adding a small amount of boiling water to the pot.

• When serving iced tea, dip the rim of the glass in lemon juice and then into a saucer filled with lemon-flavored gelatin granules or granulated sugar so that an attractive crusty edge is built up around the edge of the glass. Pour in the tea carefully so as not to ruin the effect.

• On a sweltering hot day, top iced tea with a scoop of fruit sherbet, milk ice, or ice cream balanced on the rim of the glass.

• Use a long stalk of fennel as a fragrant garnish for iced tea.

• For more intense flavor, make ice cubes from brewed tea or fruit juice and use in iced tea. When the ice melts, the tea will not become diluted.

• Insert skewered chunks of fresh fruit, such as whole strawberries, pineapple chunks, and cubed melon, into each glass of iced tea.

• Insert the stem of a single flower blossom, such as a black-eyed Susan, into the straw placed in a glass of iced tea. (Remove flower before sipping!)

• Freeze fresh mint leaves, citrus slices, or whole berries in ice cube trays filled with partially frozen water. Use the decorative cubes to chill iced tea or other tall drinks, such as lemonade, daiquiris, spritzers (wine and soda water), or mint juleps.

• Stemmed balloon or oversized goblet-shaped wineglasses make pretty containers for iced tea.

Vegetable Fillips

• Quarter a large baked acorn squash. Hollow a cavity in each quarter and fill with broccoli purée.

• Slice baked acorn squash into 1-inch-thick rings. Hollow the centers and fill with green peas.

• Bake apple-pie filling in halved acorn squash. Top with cooked crumbled pork sausage meat.

• Stuff the cavities of large sautéed mushroom caps with tiny garden peas or mashed rutabaga piped through a pastry tube. Use as a garnish around a roast loin of pork. Place small bundles of steamed green beans between the mushroom caps to set them apart.

• Serve mashed carrots in the hollowed cavities of baked summer squash, cut in half lengthwise.

• Serve diced pimiento mixed with cooked corn kernels in the hollowed cavities of lightly steamed whole zucchini squash, cut in half lengthwise.

• Cut a cross in the top of a baked potato and puff it up. Season with salt and pepper and add a heaping teaspoon of butter. When melted, squish each potato open very wide and stuff with a scoop of salmon salad. Garnish with dill sprigs.

• Stuff several baked potatoes with sour cream. Top half the potatoes with a generous sprinkling of fresh chopped chives; top the other half with a dollop of red lumpfish caviar. Arrange the potatoes on a red platter, alternating the green and the red toppings.

• Fill large onions, peeled and partially hollowed, with bread stuffing or seasoned ground beef. Bake until cooked through.

• Serve creamed peas and pearl onions in the hollowed cavities of peeled large Spanish onions that have been previously baked.

• Peel large cucumbers in stripes, then hollow out the centers with a zucchini corer (Chapter 2). Fill with salmon mousse and chill thoroughly. Cut into ½-inch slices and serve with tomato wedges and hard-cooked egg wedges arranged in a decorative pattern on a large green plate.

- Serve petits pois (little peas) in the hollow of a Boston lettuce leaf. Garnish with a sprig of mint.

- Stuff green bell peppers with macaroni and cheese for a new flavor treat.

- Stuff hollowed red bell peppers with bright green garden peas.

- A small hollowed red or green bell pepper makes an amusing container for salad dressing or mayonnaise. Stand it in the center of a plate surrounded by a mixture of salad greens, quartered radishes, and sliced raw mushrooms.

- Separate the stalks from a head of celery. Wash, trim, and remove the strings. Stuff with a mixture of cream cheese, chopped walnuts, chopped dates, and chopped mint. Reassemble the celery stalks, pressing so that the bunch is back to its original shape. Chill thoroughly. Slice into ¾-inch rounds and serve the pinwheel celery slices on a red plate, garnishing the center of each slice with a rose made from the peelings of tomatoes.

- Stuff hollowed cherry tomatoes with tuna salad and garnish each with a snippet of parsley.

- Stuff hollowed tomatoes with a cold rice salad mixture.

- Serve a whole stuffed cabbage for a spectacular-looking meal. Remove and reserve the tough outer leaves, then with a sharp knife carefully cut out the stem and center of cabbage, leaving a 1-inch-thick shell. Discard stem and chop cut-out cabbage. Sauté the cut up cabbage and combine 1 cup of it with 1 pound of cooked and seasoned ground beef and 1 cup of cooked rice. Fill cabbage with the meat mixture and place the reserved outer cabbage leaves over the opening. With string, tie cabbage securely to hold the leaves in place. Place remaining cut-up cabbage in a 5-quart Dutch oven with 1 quart of tomato sauce and the tied cabbage. Simmer until tender, about 1½ hours. To serve: place cabbage on a large round white plate and remove string. Top with tomato sauce and sprinkle with chopped parsley.

- Cut baked potatoes in half lengthwise and remove the potato with a spoon, reserving it for another use (see below). Fill baked potato shells with creamed spinach.

• Besides being used for hashed browns, the insides of baked potatoes can be made into potato pancakes, potato bread, potato soup, potato stuffing, potato dumplings, potato croquettes. Or just mash them up, season with butter, sour cream, or cheese, or mix them with a puréed root vegetable, such as turnips, rutabaga, or mashed carrots. Serve them as is or stuff them back into the hollowed skins.

• Halve and scoop out baked potatoes, reserving the insides for another use (see above). Deep-fry the shells until crisp and drain well on paper towels. Fill with chili topped with grated cheddar cheese or cottage cheese mixed with diced celery and scallions. Place the skins on a baking sheet and put back in the oven for several minutes, until heated through.

• Cut the skin off raw potatoes into strips with a small sharp knife. Soak the peelings in cold water for 30 minutes, drain well, and pat dry with paper towels. Deep-fry the peelings in hot vegetable oil or rendered beef fat, turning with a slotted spoon until they are crisp. Drain and arrange the hot potato strips on a paper doily. Serve with a bowl of warmed horseradish sauce on the side, for dipping. The peeled potatoes may be boiled and mashed or reserved for another use, if covered with ice water.

• A platter of vegetables steamed just until they're crisp-tender, then finished off with a variety of flavored butters (see Chapter 4) is a brilliant kaleidoscope of colors, shapes, and textures that makes a stunning and satisfying appetizer, entree, side dish, or salad course depending on the appetite and the mood. The vegetables can change with the seasons. Serve them on an oval white platter to set off their vibrant colors.

For example, place two rings of honey-glazed acorn squash side by side in the center of the platter. Fill each ring with a mound of steamed and buttered brussels sprouts sprinkled with bacon bits for added flavor and texture. Surround the squash with alternating mounds of buttered carrots, broccoli flowerets, and cauliflower flowerets.

• Here's a great way to bake acorn squash by using your imagination to improvise the perfect dish for the oven—a 4-cup heatproof glass measuring pitcher. Preheat oven to 400° F. Cut off the top of a medium-sized acorn squash and scoop out the seeds. Place 2 tablespoons of honey and 2 tablespoons of butter in the cavity and stand the squash cut side up in the measuring cup. Pour about 1 inch of boiling water *around* the squash, cover with aluminum foil, and bake for about 30 minutes, until tender. Baste the top and insides of the squash occasionally with the butter and honey mixture. Slice into 1-, 1½-, or 2-inch rings before serving.

Vinegars

• Sherry, Champagne, raspberry, blueberry, cider, strawberry, tarragon, shallot, red wine—the very names of vinegars create excitement. They come in a fascinating range of flavors that can add infinite variety to your dressings, marinades, and sauces. You can experiment with different vinegars to hit upon favorite and often unexpected affinities, such as sautéed chicken breasts glazed with raspberry vinegar! Keep two or three different vinegars on hand for mouth-watering subtleties in the taste of your foods.

• Sprinkle flavored vinegars on fresh fruit: for instance, raspberry vinegar on strawberries, or blueberry vinegar on blueberries served in a cantaloupe half, or strawberry vinegar on sliced bananas.

• Sprinkle flavored vinegars on crisply cooked vegetables: raspberry vinegar on crunchy steamed brussels sprouts, or strawberry vinegar on steamed green beans. A splash of cider vinegar will give braised cabbage a lively piquancy.

• Flavored vinegars can seem excessively expensive, but it's easy to make your own. All it takes to reproduce an herb or berry vinegar is to add an herb, such as basil or tarragon, or a few berries, fresh or frozen, to a bottle of white vinegar and let them stand for two or three weeks to mellow. It's as simple as that.

• Use flavored vinegars, such as sherry, red wine, or tarragon, to marinate chicken, veal, and kebabs of lamb or beef.

• Sprinkle tarragon vinegar on swordfish steaks before cooking on an outdoor grill.

• Vary your vinegars to make interesting vinaigrettes with new taste appeal.

• A splash of vinegar can enliven soups and stir-fried foods. Try cider vinegar on french fries, sherry vinegar in lentil soup, or raspberry vinegar in stir-fried pork and shredded cabbage.

• A spoonful of fruit vinegar in sparkling water with ice makes a refreshing summer drink.

• Sprinkle sherry vinegar and a little salt over toasted pine nuts or whole blanched almonds for an exciting taste sensation.

• Blend 1 teaspoon of honey with 2 tablespoons of sherry vinegar as a dressing over a sliced orange and red onion salad.

Miscellaneous Hints

To give your foods more flavor, aroma, texture, and eye appeal:

• To garnish lettuce leaves, place sweet paprika on a piece of waxed paper and dip edges of leaves in it.

• To keep cut fruits such as apples, pears, bananas, and avocados from discoloring, sprinkle lemon, lime, or pineapple juice over them.

• To keep fish from breaking while being poached, place fish on a heatproof plate, tie in a square of cheesecloth, and lower all into a large pan of simmering water or stock.

• To cut hard-cooked eggs without breaking the yolk, use a wet knife.

• To prevent meringue on pies from shrinking, spread meringue over pie filling so that it touches the sides of pastry all around the edge. After baking, allow pie to come to room temperature before chilling in the refrigerator.

• To give doughnuts and fritters added flavor, drop a few whole cloves or a stick of cinnamon into fat while frying.

• When cooking a pot roast, used canned beef broth or consommé as the liquid in place of water. This makes the gravy taste even better.

• Ten minutes before your apple pie has finished baking, remove it from the oven and sprinkle the top with ¼ to ⅓ cup grated cheddar cheese. Return to oven and allow to finish baking.

• Top a fruit salad or frosted cake with tinted coconut. Half fill a glass jar with shredded coconut and sprinkle with a few drops of food coloring. Cover and shake vigorously. Store in the refrigerator.

5.
Eventful Ideas

No matter the time of day or the time of year, your meals can be lifted out of the ordinary if you consider the entire dining concept as well as the food. Your sensitivity and attention to details are the qualities required to turn each meal into an event awaited with anticipation. Following is a collection of ideas and suggestions covering several familiar circumstances that almost all of us experience at one time or another. Since meals are served under an unlimited variety of different conditions, it's not possible for this book to discuss every occasion. However, what is covered here should be enough to stimulate your own thinking about the many other ways in which you can improve and enliven your daily fare as well as special personal situations, events, and holiday gatherings.

Breakfast

Still considered to be the most important meal of the day, the ideal breakfast should be highly nutritious, tasty, easy to prepare, and visually attractive.

- Decant milk into a pretty bottle or pitcher.
- A presentation of mild cheeses and colorful fruit can make an almost

instant yet hearty breakfast that's beautiful too. Place a disk of creamy Brie in the center of a large red platter and surround it with: clusters of purple grapes, pear slices, clusters of green grapes, and apple slices. Repeat the fruit combination four times around the platter. Accompany with warm rolls and sliced French bread in a basket lined with a red and white checked napkin.

• Serve hot cider or apple juice in a mug with a stick of cinnamon.

• A platter of cold cuts, thinly sliced ham, and salami can be arranged the night before, covered with plastic wrap, and refrigerated ready for use first thing in the morning. Garnish the platter with whole strawberries and clusters of green and purple grapes for added color appeal.

• Keep a crock or pot of honey at room temperature and use it to add variety to your morning table. Drizzle it on toast and muffins, over cereal, and stir it into coffee or tea for a flavor boost. Use a honey dipper (see Chapter 2) for easy application.

• Serve grapefruit juice in squat transparent glasses, such as French bistro wineglasses, and garnish each with a sprig of mint.

• Arrange individual bouquets of silver dollar pancakes on a large red platter. For each serving, cluster 5 pancakes in an overlapping circular pattern. Place a dollop of yogurt in the center of each cluster and top with sliced strawberries sprinkled with fine threads of orange zest.

• Here's a twist for serving bacon. Twist 8 slices of bacon into corkscrew spirals and arrange them in a row on the rack of a broiler pan. Insert a metal skewer through each end of each slice of twisted bacon. The skewers will hold the bacon in shape so that the spirals do not unwind. Bake in a preheated 375° F. oven until browned and crisp, about 15 or 20 minutes. Drain on paper towels and remove the skewers before serving. Place 2 bacon twists in an X between 2 fried eggs or on top of scrambled eggs.

• A colorful and refreshing fruit salad makes a great way to decorate your table as well as start the day. In a mixing bowl combine 2 cups cantaloupe balls, 2 cups honeydew melon balls, and 3 kiwis, peeled and sliced crosswise. Sprinkle with the juice of ½ lime and serve the salad in a large glass bowl placed in the center of your table.

Bacon Twists

• Fry 2 slices of French toast made with square slices of white or whole wheat bread. Stack the slices and cut them from corner to corner into triangles. Arrange the triangles in overlapping slices around a serving plate and garnish with 3 strawberries in the center.

• For maximum flavor and texture, make it a habit to remove butter, preserves, and other spreads from the refrigerator early in the morning. They taste better when served at room temperature.

• Dress up your morning orange. Spread 5 segments in a fanlike pattern on a glass plate. Place a few mint sprigs at the base of the fan and scatter several fresh violet blossoms over the green leaves.

• Serve ham with melon instead of eggs for breakfast. Drape 3 rosy slices of prosciutto over a fat wedge of cantaloupe and garnish with ½ lime and an orange blossom sprig.

• Serve blueberry yogurt in your prettiest teacups with a sprig of mint and a tiny cluster of green grapes placed on the saucer.

• For a hearty and colorful breakfast, cut a honeydew melon or large cantaloupe into 6 rings. Peel and scoop out the centers. Place each ring on a plate and fill the center with cubes of cheese and salami.

• Serve dry cereal such as cornflakes or raisin bran in a soup tureen to be measured out with the soup ladle.

• For a lovely light breakfast, peel and slice an orange. Arrange the slices overlapping down the center of a large white plate. Split a bran muffin and place a half on either side of the orange slices. Garnish with 2 strawberries.

• You can use small, individual baking dishes for many things, but they're perfect for shirring eggs. Butter the inside of the dish, then, for extra flavor, cover the bottom with a little chopped ham, spinach, chopped mushrooms, or tomatoes and onion. Break in 2 eggs and top the yolks with 1 or 2 tablespoons of heavy cream and a sprinkle of salt and pepper. Bake in a preheated 350° F. oven for 10 to 15 minutes, until the eggs are cooked the way you like them. Sprinkle with finely chopped parsley or chives and serve the baking dish on top of a large plate.

• Enliven soft creamy scrambled eggs with finely diced green or red bell pepper for color and zesty flavor.

• Stuff an omelet with sliced mushrooms lightly sautéed in butter with chopped shallots and seasoned with salt and freshly ground black pepper. Top the omelet with crème fraîche and a sprinkling of finely chopped dill.

Canned Chic

For those times when unexpected guests arrive, or it's too hot to cook, or you're in a hurry, or you simply just don't feel like bothering, you can dress up many canned or packaged foods and serve them with pizzazz and flair.

• Keep a can of consommé and a tin of pâté chilled in your refrigerator. Spoon a bed of the jellied consommé onto each plate. Open the tin of pâté at both ends and push one end through the can so that the pâté comes out in a neat shape. Use a warm knife (run it under hot water) to cut the pâté into thick slices. Arrange 2 overlapping slices on each plate. Garnish with cornichons and olives and serve with toast triangles or crackers.

- Pasta and pâté make an elegant but quick meal for 4 to 6 people. Open a small, chilled can of pâté de foie gras and cut it into small cubes with a warm knife. Set aside. Sauté 6 sliced black olives and a 1-pound can of drained, sliced mushrooms (or 1 pound fresh sliced mushrooms) in ½ cup of butter and season with salt and pepper. Boil 1 pound of linguine or thin spaghetti until just tender (al dente). Drain and toss with the sautéed mushrooms. Add the pâté and toss gently so as not to crush the cubes. Serve hot on large plates and sprinkle with minced parsley for added color and flavor.

- Canned tamales can be found in the Spanish section of your supermarket. Heat tamales thoroughly and remove the wrappers. Arrange on a bed of shredded lettuce and sprinkle with grated cheddar cheese. Garnish tamales with strips of pimiento and scatter black olives around the edge of the plate.

- Keep a cup of sour cream and a small jar of lumpfish caviar chilled in the refrigerator. Cook 1 pound of elbow macaroni just until tender, cool under cold running water, and drain. Place in a large bowl and toss with the sour cream and caviar. Sprinkle with thinly sliced scallions.

- For each serving, unmold 1 cup of chilled plain yogurt in the center of a shallow soup plate. Spike chilled tomato juice with a few drops of hot pepper sauce, Worcestershire sauce, and lemon juice. Surrounded the yogurt with the tomato juice and sprinkle with finely chopped green bell pepper or chopped cucumber for added color, flavor, and texture. Season with chopped chives, salt, and freshly ground black pepper.

- Place a drained small can of tuna or salmon in the center of a large glass bowl filled a third of the way with chopped or torn salad greens. Place 2 crossed anchovy fillets on top of the fish and sprinkle with a spoonful of capers. Garnish this salad with olives, cherry tomatoes, and wedges of hard-cooked egg. Serve with mayonnaise or your favorite salad dressing on the side.

- Keep a can of corned beef hash chilled in the refrigerator. Open the can at both ends and push through one end so that the corned beef comes out in a perfect cylinder. Cut into ½-inch round slices with a warm knife and fry in a non-stick pan, turning once, until browned. Serve the corned beef rounds on top of toasted English muffins and top with poached or fried eggs sprinkled with cheddar cheese.

Children's Meals

Children are notorious for going through stages and their eating habits usually change with time. They're often stubborn when it comes to likes and dislikes, and many parents may find themselves at a loss when it comes to pleasing them at mealtime. Allowing your children to assist you in the kitchen is not only fun for everyone involved but is also a good way of stimulating their interest in food. Naturally, you'll have to think of fun chores they'll take a liking to. Shaping hamburger patties and meat balls, tearing the lettuce leaves for a salad, cutting out cookie dough, and frosting cupcakes are just some examples of pleasant tasks that youngsters might find appealing. In addition, the suggestions listed here can be used to increase your children's enjoyment of food and make eating almost as amusing as a new toy.

• For sandwiches with fun appeal, use cookie cutters to make fancy shapes out of cheese slices, cold cuts, and bread. For example, place a cheese star on top of a buttered circle of bread and top with a salami heart. Or serve a gingerbread ham man on top of a buttered bread rectangle. Use a sharp knife to cut out cheese clothes (trousers, skirts, shirts, hats, neckties, etc.) to dress the ham.

• Provide each child with a plate holding an apple stuck full of miniature sandwiches on toothpicks. Make sandwiches out of thinly sliced white, whole wheat, or raisin bread; spread with preserves, peanut butter, cheese, honey, or the filling suggestions in Chapter 4. Cut each sandwich into 1-inch squares, thread 2 squares on each toothpick, and stick into the apple so it looks like a sputnik.

• Serve a french fried potato chain. Cut raw potatoes into ¼-inch slices and soak in cold water for 30 minutes. Cut a ring from each slice with a small round cookie or aspic cutter. Cut a slit in 1 ring and slip in 2 rings, making a chain of 3 links.

• For a flavor treat with eye appeal, instead of using white potatoes, serve golden french fried sweet potatoes in a blue plastic mug or a red plastic tumbler.

• Turn bananas into a special treat. Peel and cut in half crosswise; insert an ice cream stick into the cut end. Freeze bananas, then dip in pancake syrup. If you're just making 1 or 2, use a small basting brush or spoon the syrup over the pops. Roll the coated banana in chopped nuts, granola, cookie crumbs, or wheat germ. Return to freezer in a covered plastic container.

• Mix pancake batter in a container with a spout, such as a 1-quart glass measuring cup. Pour batter onto the hot griddle in interesting shapes, such as rabbits, cats, stars, or flowers.

• Let your children concoct their own ice cream sundaes for dessert. Set out bowls, spoons, and napkins. Assemble your ice cream parlor on a tray containing: assorted flavors of ice cream and sherbet; chocolate syrup, coffee syrup, maple syrup, crushed pineapple; whipped topping. Garnishes: cherries, chopped walnuts, rainbow sprinkles, wheat germ, chocolate shot, crushed peanut brittle, shredded coconut, miniature marshmallows, crushed peppermint candy.

Diet Delights

Since few people enjoy being on a diet, restricted meals require special consideration. An attractive setting and food that looks appealing even though it has its limitations can do much to bolster a dieter's spirits and offer encouragement at mealtime. The following ideas have been developed with this purpose in mind and can be used to turn a dieter's dilemma into a happier experience.

• Get fancy with flowers, candles, crystal, and china. Create a fantasy table setting that is much more satisfying than rich sauces or mountains of food. Use the best of everything you have so that you are surrounded with beautiful objects that make you feel pampered and wonderful, and not deprived by meager portions of food.

• Since it can be eaten very slowly, serving a whole artichoke at the start of a minuscule meal is a clever way of prolonging time at the table and making it more of an event for conversation.

• Velvety cold soups, luminous consommés, and sparkling madrilène acquire elegance when served in shallow crystal bowls. For an extra pretty effect, insert a leaf from the garden between the crystal bowl and the service plate.

• Drinking vegetable juice is more fun if it is served in a stemmed crystal goblet or oversized brandy snifter with a celery, cucumber, or scallion swizzle-stick garnish.

• A layered pousse-café of marinated vegetables, like a rainbow of colors, is as interesting to look at as it is to eat when served in a sparkling glass bowl that will show off its beauty. Try arranging colorful layers of marinated broccoli flowerets, carrot coins, cauliflower flowerets, wax beans, and red bell pepper strips, for example, in a clear glass soufflé dish.

• Serve colorful fresh fruits, such as a halved nectarine, a small cluster of seedless green grapes, and 3 Bing cherries on a bed of ice cubes in individual dessert bowls. The fruit will be cool and refreshing and the portion will appear to be much larger.

• Present an array of mixed crisp vegetable spears—carrots, cucumbers, zucchini, yellow squash, and scallions—packed upright in a crystal bowl of crushed ice. Nestle a bowl of curry dip in the center of the arrangement.

• Scoops of cottage cheese topped with crushed fresh pineapple or strawberries becomes a fanciful dessert when served in ice cream sundae dishes.

• Turn lunch into an extravaganza by serving a scoop of cottage cheese in a crystal compote dish placed on a green plate. Cut a nectarine into 8 wedges and press them upright (skin side out) into the cheese. Poke a trimmed scallion into the center of the cheese, shredding the green leaves to resemble a palm tree.

• Cut a honeydew melon into 6 rings. Peel and scoop out each ring. Arrange the melon rings on crystal plates covered with watercress and fill the centers with raspberries and seedless red grapes.

• With a perfect slice of poached fish, serve a sautéed fruit garnish, such as mango slices or a pineapple ring, instead of hollandaise or mayonnaise.

• Section a grapefruit or orange and toss the segments with a modicum of sweet wine or liqueur. Serve in crystal bowls or compote dishes. Garnish with a few shreds of grated rind and a sprig of mint.

• A light sprinkling of flavored vinegar, such as raspberry or sherry, a sparse grating of hard cheese, or a faint dusting of nutmeg makes a flavorful substitution for butter on vegetables.

- On meat, try a splash of wine or a few drops of soy sauce instead of calorie-laden gravy.

- Slice your intake of food with a sharp knife. Less becomes more when ingredients are reduced to bite size. Shredded lettuce, cabbage, and/or carrots, for example, can make a small salad look more substantial. Cubed Cheddar cheese and apple slices on a large plate make a meal of the minuscule.

- Cut away the flowerets from cauliflower or broccoli. Cut the stalks (peel broccoli stalk first) into julienne strips. Steam the pieces for 5 minutes, then add the flowerets and continue cooking until tender, about 5 minutes longer. Sprinkle lightly with sherry vinegar instead of butter or sauce, and serve at room temperature.

- Instead of buying individual steaks, buy one large piece of meat and carve it. A few thin slices of meat fanned on a plate along with a lettuce wedge and two whole beets will provide both the appeal and the nourishment you need to sustain you for the evening.

- For dessert, cut a thin slice from a regular slice of pie or cake. Garnish with a whole strawberry for added eye appeal.

- Cut down on salt and experiment with colorful fresh herbs, such as chopped basil, mint, and dill, and seasonings such as hot pepper sauce, curry powder, and chili powder to boost flavor and eye appeal of your foods. A very light dusting of coriander, for example, on green beans will raise them to new culinary heights.

- Don't serve everything on the plate at the same time. Offer a selection of appropriate foods in different courses—variety is satisfying, not quantity. For example, serve a small salad—a few sprigs of watercress with sliced radishes—either before or after the main course. Serve a lamb chop and a sautéed mushroom cap stuffed with tiny peas as one course, and half a baked potato topped with yogurt and chopped chives as a separate course.

- Learn to take a somewhat oriental view of food and enjoy smaller portions of food that are enhanced by interesting textures and flavors as well as design. For example, arrange 3 Bibb lettuce leaves in a row on one side of a large white plate, 4 slices of refreshing scarlet-tinged nectarines on the opposite side of the plate, and line 4 cubes of blue cheese, soft and crumbly, to balance the visual picture as well as create wonderful taste sensations.

• The hollow of a halved peach or nectarine is just the right cup for a miniaturized offering of sherbet. Island the fruit in a tiny pond of crushed strawberries for added color and flavor.

• When there's a glaring vacancy on a dieter's plate caused by the omission of a prohibited food, fill in the space with a special something, such as a solitary flower blossom, a fluted mushroom cap perched atop two baby spinach leaves, or a sculpted radish rose nested in a bramble of alfalfa sprouts.

• Store a see-through glass jar containing a medley of marinated vegetables in the refrigerator to tempt covert midnight nibblers away from other prohibited foods. Water-packed fruits, such as mandarin oranges and pineapple chunks, can also be on display in clear containers.

• In a small bowl with an electric mixer, whip an amount of unsalted butter until smooth. Gradually beat in half its quantity of water or an equal quantity of buttermilk until totally blended. If desired, season with chopped fresh herbs, such as chives, dill, or parsley, or with crushed strawberries or pineapple. Pack into a crock, cover, and chill. Soften slightly before serving.

Invalid Meals

Poor health is often accompanied by a loss of appetite. This is especially true if a sick person is placed on a bland and uninteresting diet. Trying to make such meals look appealing can be a real challenge. There's not much you can do to enhance the surroundings if a person is confined to bed. So you will have to rely on using your wits to create a meal tray that's as attractive as possible. Here are a few suggestions:

• Give the tray a new look for each meal by varying your choice of place mats and napkins. You might, for example, use a cheery yellow and white checked pattern for breakfast, a pale blue floral print for lunch, and a lacy mat with a brightly colored napkin for dinner.

• Use your best glassware, plates, and cutlery to make the tray look special.

- If there's room on the tray, arrange a nosegay of colorful flowers such as violets and lilies of the valley in a crystal liqueur glass or in your prettiest demitasse cup.

- Set a miniature book of poetry on an afternoon tray of tea.

- Cheerful reading matter placed alongside the breakfast tray makes a pleasant way to start the day. Depending on the age and gender of the person who's ill, roll up a comic book, a booklet of paper dolls, the sports page or fashion page of the daily newspaper, and tie it with a brightly colored bow.

- If you're serving toast, cut each slice into 4 triangles and arrange the pieces in a decorative overlapping pattern. Garnish with a perfect solitary strawberry, if permitted in the diet.

- If medicine must accompany the food, serve it with imagination. Liquid medicines can be measured into a pretty liqueur glass and pills will look far more appealing if served in the shallow well of a china egg cup.

- Finger bowls might appear ostentatious at a modern dinner party. However, they're a great way of showing an extra amount of attention to someone who's ill. For added color and flair, add a lemon twist or float a few rose petals on the water.

Hot Weather Food

You can beat the heat with splendid cold dishes that don't require any cooking. Food emporiums and delicatessens offer an astonishing array of glamorous ingredients and foods that can whet the appetite even in sweltering weather: shiny olives, smoked meats and fish, slabs of cheese, fresh bread, garden herbs and vegetables, dill, chives, basil, and juicy tomatoes or seasonal fresh fruits, such as peaches, grapes, nectarines, and melons, are all available to be arranged with imagination into colorful, sensual cold platters. Obviously, meals should be light—salads, cold meats, fruits, fresh breads, cheeses—and the refrigerator should be stocked with cold beverages, such as white wine, fizzy mineral waters, iced tea, tonic, soda, and lemons and limes for garnishes.

- On a pale blue plate arrange thin slices of cold roast beef sprinkled with freshly ground black pepper. Serve with a small bunch of watercress.

2 tomato wedges, some crumbled blue cheese, and 4 triangles of buttered rye bread. Pour a glass of slightly cooled Beaujolais for a refreshing beverage.

• Line a wicker basket with a blue paisley napkin or cotton bandana. Fill with 2 pieces of cold barbecued chicken, a fresh buttered roll, 2 stalks of celery stuffed with creamy Brie cheese, a perfect rosy peach, and a small cluster of seedless green grapes.

• Tomatoes are perfect in late summer and are wonderful sliced and overlapped down the center of a large white plate. Sprinkle with finely chopped basil, virgin olive oil, and feta cheese. Line overlapping slices of cold cooked kielbasa (Polish sausage) on both sides of the tomatoes, tucking small sprigs of watercress underneath the rows. Garnish with Mediterranean olives and serve with small buttered rounds of party rye or pumpernickel bread.

• Fresh figs are delicious and beautiful quartered and served with overlapping triangles of sliced salami. Accompany with goat cheese, olives, and a hunk of French bread, partially sliced.

• Try slices of smoked turkey arranged on a large plate with a small bunch of watercress and a dollop of horseradish sauce. Accompany with coleslaw served in an orange shell and slices of rye bread.

• Spread a slice of rye bread with cream cheese and completely cover with gravlax (salt-cured raw salmon), sliced paper-thin and sprinkled with chopped dill or chives. Serve with a wedge of lemon.

• Place 3 overlapping slices of red onion in the center of a large white plate and top with smoked herring. Place a small white dish of cucumber salad sprinkled with dill on the same plate.

• Toss slivers of tongue with julienned raw zucchini and quartered radishes in a vinaigrette dressing and serve in the cavity of an avocado half.

• Season lump crab meat with mustard and mayonnaise and serve in a lettuce cup with slices of tomato sprinkled with fresh chopped basil.

• Serve raw scallops marinated in lime juice in a crystal bowl placed on a large plate. Serve with sliced tomatoes topped with crumbled feta cheese and olives on one side of the plate.

• Arrange a few leaves of raw spinach on one side of a large plate and top with a scoop of cold rice salad. Serve with slices of cold smoked chicken and a dollop of mustardy mayonnaise.

Independence Day—Red, White, and Blue Foods

Holidays offer unique opportunities to really have fun with food. So it was decided that at least one should be included in this chapter. Of all those to choose from, you might wonder why Independence Day was singled out as the example. Actually, it was selected because of its versatility. It is the one occasion that is meaningful to every American. While other holidays might be as festive, many are steeped in family traditions and beliefs which make them very personal celebrations. The suggestions throughout this book can be used to brighten any occasion you choose, but the menu ideas listed below go one step beyond. The spirit of the holiday, as represented by the flag in this case, is amusingly expressed through the colors and names of various foods. By selecting one or more items from the headings below, you'll be able to compile a delightful menu with a theme for celebration.

Appetizers:

• Radish roses in a blue bowl

• Cold vichyssoise in a blue bowl, garnished with a tomato rose

• New England clam chowder in a blue bowl, garnished with a cherry tomato

• Cream cheese canapés topped with red lumpfish caviar

• Fruit cup of pitted Bing cherries, blueberries, and miniature marshmallows, topped with shredded coconut

Main Dish:

• Bluefish, broiled or baked

• Red snapper, broiled or baked

• Lobsters, steamed or boiled, garnished with blossoms of blue bachelor buttons

Side Dishes:

- Baked potatoes topped with sour cream and red lumpfish caviar
- Pickled beets in a white or blue bowl
- Boiled white rice flecked with red bell pepper pieces
- Sliced tomato and red onion salad served with blue cheese dressing
- Red leaf lettuce, quartered radishes, and sliced red bell pepper salad served with blue cheese dressing

Desserts:

- Vanilla ice cream or tapioca pudding topped with strawberries and blueberries
- Cherry gelatin topped with blue-tinted whipped cream
- Cherry pie topped with vanilla ice cream
- Blueberry, strawberry, or raspberry yogurt
- Red fruit compote of pitted cherries, halved purple plums, and raspberries

Beverages:

- Red and white wine
- Mineral water, soda water, strawberry soda garnished with strawberries, cherries, raspberries, or blueberries
- Cherry fruit punch

Picnics

Food may taste better when eaten outdoors, but it can be enjoyed even more if special consideration is given to its presentation. Try planning your next picnic with a bit of panache by using some of the suggestions below.

• Set your picnic on an oriental rug, a raffia mat, a patchwork quilt, or a twin-size designer sheet instead of on an old blanket.

- Use a sunny yellow pillowcase as a camouflage for a plastic wastebasket that will serve as an ice bucket. Place the basket in the pillowcase, tuck the ends inside the basket, and fill it with crushed ice. Secure the fabric by tying a yellow plaid ribbon around the basket.
- Accent your picnic table or blanket with a flowering potted plant—petunias, for example.
- Portable oil lamps, flame sheltered from the wind, are a perfect way to highlight a picnic setting.
- Create an edible centerpiece with fresh fruit (nectarines, plums, bananas, and seedless green grapes) arranged in a wicker basket.
- Glamorize your picnic table with candles sheltered from the breeze inside hurricane shades.
- Pack a picnic for one in a wooden mushroom box lined with a red checked linen towel.
- Pack marinated vegetables in old-fashioned glass canning jars that will show off the beauty of their vivid colors—orange carrots, green beans, pearl onions, and yellow corn kernels.
- Use hollowed fruit shells, such as grapefruit halves, lined with lettuce leaves as disposable containers for portions of chicken or tuna salad.
- Serve fruit salad in disposable hollowed melon halves. Be sure to leave enough melon lining to help the shell retain a firm shape.
- If you have an open fire, serve colorful kebabs for dessert: alternate marshmallows, cubes of poundcake, and pineapple chunks on a skewer and grill until lightly browned.
- For each person, roll a knife, a fork, and a spoon inside a terry hand towel and tie securely with a matching ribbon. The flatware bundles will be easy to pack and the hand towels make giant-sized napkins.
- A stacked oriental basket is a handy carryall for small edibles, such as individual quiches or fruit tarts, hors d'oeuvre, or candy—individual foods or dishes go in separate compartments that fit atop each other.
- Stuff a whole French or Italian loaf, partially hollowed, with pâté or a Spanish omelet; slice, then wrap whole in aluminum foil. Serve as sandwiches.

Wine and Cheese Tasting

Everyone loves a party. But these days the cost of entertaining can really take a generous bite out of a budget. One solution is to plan a gathering around a wine and cheese tasting. There are many fine wines available that will cost you far less than if you were to serve cocktails or mixed drinks. If you feel that you don't know enough about buying wine, most wine shop and package store dealers will be pleased to help you select two or more reasonably priced jugs and will also help you calculate the quantity you'll need for the size of your guest list. Some folks are nicer than others, so if you don't find a cooperative clerk at the first store you visit, try another. When shopping for cheese, you may notice that the price can vary to a great degree. If necessary, look in several stores for the best values and try to find weekly specials at a discount. Buy some fresh seasonal fruit, some crackers and long loaves of bread, and you will then have the makings for an event that will prove to be as much of a learning experience as it is an enjoyable evening. Conversation will flow as guests compare their preferences. The ideas listed below will help you set the stage.

• Use a white tablecloth which can serve as a background when people hold their glasses against it to look at the wine's color and depth. A wooden table top also makes a charming background.

• Use empty wine bottles from a previous tasting as holders for candles. Place these randomly over the table. The flickering flames will highlight all the glassware.

• Avoid floral centerpieces because their aroma will conflict with that of the wine and cheese. Instead create a spectacular centerpiece from leaves and fruits. Arrange a potted grape ivy plant in the center of the table with its branches trailing over the cloth. Surround it with polished red and green apples, small clusters of grapes, and whole walnuts placed directly on the cloth.

• Provide each guest with 2 large, stemmed, transparent wineglasses—one for white wine and one for red. Set out a pitcher of water so that guests can rinse their glasses after tasting each wine. Set out a large receptacle, such as a stainless steel bucket, to collect the rinse water. Dress it up by tying a red ribbon around it.

• Place several different cheeses on boards or straw mats with a separate knife or spreader for each. If possible, line the boards and mats with fresh grape or citrus leaves. Label each cheese, for increased enjoyment and conversation. The labels needn't be elaborate. In fact your children can make them—just a 3-inch triangle cut out of cardboard, either stuck gently into the top of the cheese or laid beside it, with the name printed in block letters. Garnish with small clusters of grapes and whole strawberries.

• Offer thinly sliced French bread, melba toast, sesame sticks, crisp unsalted crackers, and sliced pumpernickel from wicker bread baskets lined with red napkins.

• Provide each guest with a small white plate, a fruit knife and fork, and a napkin arranged at each setting or at one end of the table if you prefer buffet style.

• When presenting a glass of wine, *never* fill it more than a third to a half full. Those who appreciate wine need the extra space at the top of the glass so that they can swirl the wine without spilling it—the swirling action releases the bouquet of the wine and all its aromas.

Meals for One

Glamorous-looking food lifts depression and swells the spirits to new heights. A meal for one person can be turned into a creative event and an uplifting time of day. One can indulge in more expensive foods, such as shrimp, smoked trout, and lamb chops, that might otherwise be too expensive, and they can be prepared any way that you like them without having to consider other people's likes or dislikes. This is one time when you can truly give way to your fancies and have fun with food.

• Sprinkle shredded smoked salmon into scrambled eggs and stir until cooked to the desired consistency. Serve on a large plate edged with buttered toast points.

• Slip a half dozen shucked oysters into a pan of simmering light cream and cook just until the edges of the oysters begin to curl. Transfer to a red soup plate and top with a pat of butter, a sprinkle of sweet paprika, and some finely chopped parsley.

• Serve sautéed veal scaloppine on a large white plate accompanied by green linguine capped with a verdant pesto sauce. Mate with a red wine such as a Spanna or Chianti poured into your best stemmed glassware.

• Serve sautéed soft-shelled crabs on toast spread with tartar sauce. Place the open sandwich on a large plate garnished with a lemon wedge and a sprig of dill. Sprinkle chopped dill over the crab for added color and flavor.

• Dress a warm salad of equal portions of steamed whole green beans, strips of sautéed calf's liver, and diced raw avocado with a vinaigrette dressing made with sherry vinegar and virgin olive oil. Sprinkle with toasted sesame seeds and serve on a large glass plate.

• Place a broiled swordfish steak on a large white plate and top with a pat of butter and a sprig of fresh tarragon. Accompany with a baked potato skin filled with creamed spinach.

• Stuff a half dozen large mushroom caps with drained, canned snails and garlic butter. Bake in a preheated 350° F. oven for about 25 minutes, until tender and bubbly. Serve on a large plate surrounded by buttered toast points, sprinkled with finely chopped parsley. Indulge yourself with a split of chilled Champagne, if desired.

Index

Ambiance, *ix*
Antimacassars as napery, 66
Antique quilts as napery, 65
Apple corer, 16
Apple divider, **16–17**
Aromas, *ix*, 2
Aspic cutter, 17–19
Avocado and egg for rolled sandwich filling, 124–25

Baba mold, 50
Bacon and chicken liver for rolled sandwich filling, 124
Banana and peanut butter for rolled sandwich filling, 125
Bandanas as napkins, 68
Baskets, other uses for, 79–80
Beach towels as napery, 65
Beef stew, presentation of, 7
Beige fruits, 10
Beige vegetables, 10
Big appleburger, 110
Bird's nest maker, 19–20
Bishop's hat (napkin fold), 72
Black fruits, 10
Black vegetables, 10
Blue fruits, 9
Blue vegetables, 9
Body-beautiful farms, *xii*
Boning knife, 59, 61
Bottles, other uses for, 80
Bouquet garni bags, 20
Bowls
  other uses for, 80–82
  serving, preheated covered, 2
Brandy snifters, other uses for, 86–87
Bread, presentation of, 93

Bread cubes, toasted, as salad topping, 122
Breakfast, 139–42
Breakfast butters, 94
Breakfast cereals as salad topping, 122
Breakfast frank, 102
Breakfast in bed, *xii*
Brioche mold, 50–51
Brown fruits, 10
Brown vegetables, 10
Brushes, mushroom, 32–33
Buffet server (napkin fold), 70
Bug bulbs, yellow, 14
Burger queen, 110
Butter, presentation of, 93–95
Butter curlers, 20
Butter molds, 54
Butter paddles, 20

Cake plates, other uses for, 82
Cakes, presentation of, 95–96
California burger, 110
Canadian burger, 110
Canapé butters, 94
Canapé spreaders, 76
Candle (napkin fold), 69
Candleholders, 12–13
Candles, 12–13
Canned foods, dressing up, 142–43
Canned fruit as salad topping, 122
Canned vegetables
  presentation of, 8
  as salad topping, 122
Cappuccino, 99
Carafes, other uses for, 83
Carrot curls, 106
Carving knife, 61

Index

Casseroles, presentation of, 97
Caviar, 10, 11
Celery curls, 106
Centerpiece ideas, 76–78
Ceramic tiles as place settings, 67
Cereals as salad topping, 122
Chafing dishes, other uses for, 83
Checkerboard finger sandwiches, 126–27
Cheese
  presentation of, 7
  as salad topping, 123
  and wine tasting party, 154–55
Cheese cubes for skewered salads, 120
Cheese graters, 27
Chef's knife, 15, 59, 60–61
Chef's salad, 101
Cherry pitter, 22
Chicken
  improving texture of, 4
  for rolled sandwich filling, 124
Chicken liver and bacon for rolled sandwich filling, 124
Children's meals, 144–45
Chocolate, presentation of, 97–98
Chocolate leaves, 98
Citronella candles, 14
Citrus peelings, 2
Citrus scorer and stripper, 23
Citrus sheller, 23–24
Citrus shells, scalloped, 39–40
Citrus wedges, 105
Citrus zester, 24
Club sandwiches, 127–28
Coeur à la crème, 48–49
Coffee, presentation of, 99
Coffee cubes, 111
Coffeepots, other uses for, 83
Colanders, other uses for, 84
Cold cuts for skewered salads, 120
Color chart, cook's, 8–11
Colorful edibles as table accessories, 5
Colors, *ix, x,* 5–11
Comfort, *ix*
Condiments, presentation of, 100
Containers, *x*
Conviviality, *ix*
Cookie jars, other uses for, 84–85
Cook's color chart, 8–11
Corers
  apple, 16
  zucchini, 47
Corn on the cob, presentation of, 7
Cotton rugs as napery, 65
Creamers, other uses for, 90
Croque monsieur toasting iron, 55
Croutons as salad topping, 122

Cucumber with tuna or salmon for rolled sandwich filling, 125
Culinary molds, 48–58
Cutters
  for aspic, garnishing, and truffles, 17–19
  melon ball, 31–32
  pineapple, 38–39
  radish spiral, 40–41
  tomato, 44
Cutting boards, other uses for, 85

Décor, *ix*
Deli burger, 111
Demitasse cups and saucers, other uses for, 83–84
Demitasse spoons, 76
Dessert butters, 94
Desserts, coeur à la crème, 48–49
Diet meals, dressing up, 145–48
Dimmers, 14
Dinner plates, 74
Dippers, honey, 28
Dividers, apple and pear, 16–17
Dixie dog, 102
Double diamonds (napkin fold), 70
Dried fruits as salad topping, 122
Dutch franks, 101

Edibles, colorful, as table accessories, 5
Egg and avocado for rolled sandwich filling, 124–25
Egg cups, other uses for, 85
Egg en gelée ramekins, 51
Egg rings, 24
Eggs
  presentation of, 8
  as salad topping, 123
Egg salad for rolled sandwich filling, 125
Egg slicer, 26
Egg wedger, 26

Favorite burger, 111
Finger sandwiches, checkerboard, 126–27
Fireplaces, 14
Fish
  improving texture of, 4
  presentation of, 8, 100–1, 112–13
  as salad topping, 122–23
  for skewered salads, 120
Flatware, 75–78
Flavor combinations, *x*
Floral printed napkins, 68
Flower butters, 95

Index   159

Flowers
  as food garnish, 109
  with napkins, 68
  seasonal, 5
Fluted knife, 62
Fluter, mushroom, 33–34
Food preparation, 4
Food presentation, *x*, 92–138
  bread, 93
  butter, 93–95
  cakes, 95–96
  casseroles, 97
  cheese, 7
  chocolate, 97–98
  coffee, 99
  condiments, 100
  eggs, 8
  fish, 8, 100–1, 112–13
  frankfurters, 101–2
  fruits, 8, 102–4
  garnishes, 104–9
  hamburgers, 110–11
  ice, 111–12
  margarine, 93–95
  meat, 7, 112–13
  miscellaneous hints, 138
  oils, 113
  pastry dough, 114
  pie crimping, 114–16
  potatoes, 7, 116–17
  poultry, 112–13
  rice, 117–18
  salads, 118–21
  salad toppings, 121–23
  sandwiches, 123–31
  soups, 132
  teas, 132–33
  vegetables, 8, 134–36
  vinegars, 137–38
Frankfurters, presentation of, 101–2
Frankly delightful, 102
Franks espagnole, 101–2
French franks, 101
Fresh fruits as salad topping, 122
Fresh herbs as salad topping, 122
Fresh vegetables as salad topping, 122
Frisbees as paper plate holders, 75
Frosted fruits, 106
Frosted sandwich cake, 131
Fruit forks, 76
Fruit juice cubes, 111–12
Fruit knives, 76
Fruits
  beige, 10
  black, 10
  blue, 9
  brown, 10
  as candleholders, 12
  frosted, 106
  green, 9
  orange, 10
  presentation of, 8, 102–4
  purple, 9
  red, 10
  as salad topping, 122
  for skewered salads, 120
  white, 11
  yellow, 10

Gadgets for kitchen use, 16–47
Garden dog, 102
Garlic, 2
Garnishes
  presentation of, 104–9
  as salad topping, 122
Garnishing cutter, 17–19
Gelatin molds, 56
Glasses, other uses for, 86–87
Glass panes as place settings, 67
Glazed franks, 101
Grapefruit, presentation of, 8
Grapefruit knife, 62–63
Grapes, scissors for, 75
Graters, 27
Greek burger, 110
Greenery, minced, suggested uses for, 42
Green fruits, 9
Green herbs, 9
Green vegetables, 8–9
Grinders, 27

Hamburgers
  improving texture of, 4
  presentation of, 110–11
Handy burger, 110
Hawaiian burger, 110
Health consciousness, *xii*
Herb butters, 94
Herbs, 2, 3
  fresh, as salad topping, 122
  green, 9
Hog dog, 102
Holiday menus, 151–52
Homemade place mats, 66–67
Honey dipper, 28
Hot weather food, 149–51
Hullers, strawberry, 43
Hurricane lamps, 12, 14

Ice, presentation of, 111–12
Ice buckets, other uses for, 87
Ice cream molds, 56

Index

Ice cream scoops, 28–29
Ice cube tongs, 76
Ice sculpture molds, 52
Independence Day menu, 151–52
Indian burger, 111
Individual molds, 49–50
International burger, 110
Intruding smells, 2
Invalid meals, *xii*
   dressing up, 148–49
Irish linen dish toweling as napkins, 68
Italian burger, 111

Julienne vegetables, 107

Kitchen equipment, *x,* 15–63
   culinary molds, 48–58
   gadgets, 16–47
   knives, 15, 59–63
   tools, 16–47
Knives, 15, 59–63

Lace tablecloths, 65
Layered salads, 120–21
Lemons, 2
Lemon wedge bags, 30
Light bulbs, 14
   pink, 14
   yellow bug, 14
Lighting, *x,* 12–14

Macaroni and frank salad, 101
Margarine, presentation of, 93–95
Meals for one, *xi–xii*
Meat
   presentation of, 7, 112–13
   for rolled sandwich filling, 125
   as salad topping, 122
   for skewered salads, 120
Meat frills, 30
Meat loaf molds, 56–58
Melon ball cutters, 31–32
Men, food-related activities and, *xi*
Mills, 27
Minced greenery, suggested uses of, 42
Mincer, rolling, 42
Mineral water cubes, 111
Miniature sandwiches, 128–29
Mirrors as place settings, 66
Molds, culinary, 48–58
Mushroom brush, 32–33
Mushroom fluter, 33–34

Napery, 5, 65–73
   guide to folding napkins, 69–73
New England burger, 110

Nuts, 10, 11
   as salad topping, 121

Oil lamps, 14
Oils, 113
Olive pitter, 22
One-parent families, *xi*
Onion chrysanthemums, 107
Open-face sandwiches, 129–31
Orange butterflies, 107–8
Orange fruits, 10
Orange loops, 109
Orange vegetables, 10
Outdoor lighting for alfresco dining, 14

Packaged foods, dressing up, 142–43
Palm-frond fans as place settings, 67
Paper doilies, 66
Paper plates, 75
Paring knives, 15
Parties, cheese and wine tasting, 154–55
Pastry bags, 34–36
Pastry dough, presentation of, 114
Pastry wheels, 36
Pâté molds, 56–58
Patio lights, 14
Peanut butter and banana for rolled
   sandwich filling, 125
Pear divider, 16–17
Peelers, vegetable, 4, 15, 45–46
Pepper mills, 27
Pickle fans, 105
Pickles as salad topping, 122
Picnics, 152–53
Pie bird, 37
Pie crimping, 114–16
Pie spatula, 37
Pie weights, 38
Pineapple and chicken for rolled
   sandwich filling, 124
Pineapple cutter, 38–39
Pink light bulbs, 14
Pinwheel sandwiches, 126
Pita franks, 102
Pitchers, other uses for, 87–88
Pitters, cherry and olive, 22
Pizza burger, 111
Pizza franks, 101
Place mats, 5, 66
   homemade, 66–67
   tablecloths and, 65
Plates
   cake, other uses for, 82
   color and, 6
Plate service, 73–75
Platters, other uses for, 88

Index 161

Pork, improving texture of, 4
Potato and frank salad, 101
Potatoes
  improving texture of, 4
  presentation of, 7, 116–17
Potato salad, presentation of, 7–8
Poultry, presentation of, 112–13
Preheated, covered serving bowls, 2
Punch bowl set, other uses for, 88–89
Purple fruits, 9
Purple vegetables, 9

Rabbit ears (napkin fold), 69
Radish roses, 105
Radish rosette press, 39–40
Radish spiral cutter, 40–41
Ramekins for egg en gelée, 51
Red fruits, 10
Red vegetables, 9
Red wine butter, 95
Reuben burger, 110
Rheostats, 14
Ribbons as napery, 66
Rice, presentation of, 117–18
Rings, egg, 24
Ring-shaped molds, 53
Rolled sandwiches, 123–25
Rolling mincer, 42
Russian burger, 110

Salads, presentation of, 118–21
Salad toppings, 121–23
Salmon with cucumber for rolled sandwich filling, 125
Sandwiches
  presentation of, 123–31
  toasting iron for, 55
Savarin molds, 53
Savory butters, 94
Scalloped citrus shells, 39–40
Scallop shells, other uses for, 89–90
Scented candles, 14
Scissors for grapes, 75
Scoops, ice cream, 28–29
Scrambled burger, 110
Seashells, other uses for, 89–90
Seasonal flowers, 5
Seasoning, 3
Seeds as salad topping, 122
Serrated knife, 59, 61
Service for one (plate service), 74
Serving bowls, preheated, covered, 2
Shawls as napery, 66
Sheets as napery, 65–66
Shrimp cleaners, 43
Skewered salads, 119–20

Slicers, egg, 26
Slicing knife, 59, 61
Smells, intruding, 2
Snack butters, 94
Solid-colored napkins, 68
Sophisticated frank, 102
Soups
  improving texture of, 4
  presentation of, 132
Spanish fan (napkin fold), 73
Spatulas, pie, 37
Spices, 2, 3
Spinach burger, 111
Spreaders, canapé, 76
Sprouts as salad topping, 122
Stainless flatware, 75
Stain-resistant table toppers, 68
Stews
  beef, presentation of, 7
  improving texture of, 4
Store-bought molds, 49
Strainers, 3
Strawberry hullers, 43
Stuffed-egg plates, other uses for, 86
Sugar bowls, other uses for, 90
Sugar tongs, 76
Swiss franks, 101

Table accessories, color and, 5
Table appointments, *x*
Tablecloths, place mats and, 65
Table runners, 67
Table settings, 64–91
  flatware, 75–78
  multifunctional tableware, 79–91
  napery, 5, 65–73
    guide to folding napkins, 69–73
  plate service, 73–75
Tableware, *x*
  multifunctional, 79–91
Taco burger, 110
Tartan blankets as napery, 65
Tastes, *ix*, 3
Tea cubes, 111
Teapots, other uses for, 83
Teas, presentation of, 132–33
Terrine molds, 56–58
Terry hand towels as napkins, 68
Tex-Mex dog, 102
Textures, *ix, x,* 3–4
Timbale mold, 50
Timers, 3
Toasted bread cubes as salad topping, 122
Toasted cheese roll-ups, 123
Toasting iron for sandwiches, 55

Tomato cutter, 44
Tomato roses, 107
Tongs, 76
Tongue for rolled sandwich filling, 125
Tools for kitchen use, 16–47
Torches, 14
Towels
  as napkins, 68
  Wash'n Dri premoistened towelettes, 67
Trays as place settings, 67
Treasure chest of sandwiches, 131
Truffle cutter, 17–19
Tuna
  with cucumber for rolled sandwich filling, 125
  presentation of, 8
Tureens, other uses for, 91

Vegetable baskets, 107
Vegetable butters, 94
Vegetable cups, 105
Vegetable peelers, 4, 15, 45–46
Vegetables
  beige, 10
  black, 10
  blue, 9
  brown, 10
  as candleholders, 12
  canned, presentation of, 8
  combinations of, 7
  cooking time for, 3
  green, 8–9
  julienne, 107
  orange, 10
  presentation of, 8, 134–36
  purple, 9
  red, 9
  as salad topping, 122
  for skewered salads, 120
  white, 11
  yellow, 10
Vegetable trimmings as salad topping, 122
Vinegars, 137–38
Vinyl cloth as napery, 68
V-knife, 63
Votive candles, 12, 13

Waffle sandwiches, 126
Wash'n Dri premoistened towelettes, 67
Wedgers, egg, 26
Weights, pie, 38
White fruits, 11
White vegetables, 11
Wine and cheese tasting party, 154–55
Wine bottles as candleholders, 13
Wine butter, red, 95
Wine coolers, other uses for, 87
Wine cubes, 111
Wineglasses as candleholders, 13
Wine goblets, other uses for, 86–87
Wonderball, 46

Yellow bug bulbs, 14
Yellow fruits, 10
Yellow vegetables, 10

Zest, 24
Zester, citrus, 24
Zigzag knife, 63
Zucchini corer, 47